D1434743

WILLIAM LAMB

ANE RESONYNG

OF ANE SCOTTIS AND INGLIS MERCHAND
BETUIX ROWAND AND LIONIS

Other AUP titles of interest

SCOTLAND AND THE LOWLAND TONGUE
Edited by J Derrick McClure

SCOTTISH HANDWRITING 1150–1650
an introduction to the reading of documents
G G Simpson

GEORGE BUCHANAN Prince of Poets
Philip J Ford

A DICTIONARY OF THE OLDER SCOTTISH TONGUE
from the twelfth century to the end of the seventeenth
Edited by Sir William Craigie 1925–1955, A J Aitken 1955–,
James C Stevenson 1973–

THE SCOTTISH NATIONAL DICTIONARY
eighteenth century to present day
Edited by William Grant 1929–46, David D Murison 1946–76

WILLIAM LAMB

ANE RESONYNG

OF ANE SCOTTIS AND INGLIS MERCHAND
BETUIX ROWAND AND LIONIS

––––––––

EDITED

WITH AN INTRODUCTION, COMMENTARY
AND GLOSSARY

BY

RODERICK J LYALL

––––––––

ABERDEEN UNIVERSITY PRESS

First published 1985
Aberdeen University Press
A member of the Pergamon Group
© Roderick J Lyall 1985

The Publisher acknowledges subsidy from the
Scottish Arts Council towards the publication
of this volume.

British Library Cataloguing in Publication Data

Lamb, William
    William Lamb Ane resonyng of ane Scottis and Inglis
    merchand betuix Rowand and Lionis. 1. Scotland—Politics
    and government—16th century
    I. Title   II. Lyall, Roderick J
    941.105   DA784

    ISBN 0 08 030386 2
    ISBN 0 08 028485 X Pbk

Printed in Great Britain
The University Press
Aberdeen

CONTENTS

ACKNOWLEDGEMENTS

I am indebted to the Librarian of the British Library for access to the manuscript and for providing a microfilm of the text. It also gives me great pleasure to acknowledge the help of the many colleagues who have freely given information and advice, and especially Dr John Durkan, who read and commented upon the typescript with his characteristic acerbity; Professor Ian Cowan, who made available the unpublished materials from the Vatican Archives held on microfilm in the Department of Scottish History, University of Glasgow; Mr Tom Graham, Librarian of the University of York, who provided valuable data from those sections of the Vatican materials currently in his possession; Professor Jack Aitken and Dr James Stevenson with their colleagues in the *Dictionary of the Older Scottish Tongue*, who made available the unpublished files of the *Dictionary*; and Professor John Larner. My debt to my wife, for her tolerance and support, goes without saying, but I nevertheless acknowledge it here with great gratitude.

INTRODUCTION

THE MANUSCRIPT

The text here edited is found in a unique copy as part of British Library MS. Cotton Caligula B.vii. This is a bound album, containing for the most part Scottish correspondence of the sixteenth century, one of eight such collected by the seventeenth-century antiquarian Sir Robert Cotton.[1] Among these miscellaneous letters fols. 354^r–381^v are distinctive, consisting of a single quire of thirty leaves, of which the last eight are blank. On the rest is written the prose dialogue which is the subject of this edition, attributed on fol. 354^r to Mr William Lamb, parson of Conveth and Senator of the College of Justice. The layout of the title-page, and more particularly the reference to Lamb's 'brother', Mr Patrick Liddell, 'author that this buke is cum to knawlege of the redar', suggest that the manuscript may have been prepared for publication; and the terms of the attribution give no indication that the author of the *Resonyng* itself was no longer alive. It follows, therefore, that this copy must have been made before the summer of 1550, by which time Lamb was certainly dead. These inferences are consistent with the topical nature of the text, which would have justified publication in the early part of 1550, but not thereafter.[2]

There is no mistaking the care with which this Cotton manuscript of the *Resonyng* was prepared. Various errors and omissions indicate that it was not an authorial original, but the presence of frequent marginal and interlinear additions and emendations in the scribe's own hand testifies to scrupulous preparation. The eight blank leaves at the end of the quire raise the question whether there was ever another portion of the *Resonyng*, which the scribe intended to add but never did. The opening pages of Lamb's work suggest that there will be a discussion of both Henry VIII's *Declaracion* and Protector Somerset's *Exhortacion to vnitie and peace* (5/11–7/5), and the closing words on fol. 375ᵛ indicate that a refutation of the latter book will follow. Yet at this point the text breaks off. It certainly seems likely that the eight empty leaves were originally intended to carry this promised continuation, but that Lamb never completed his work. Perhaps, as has recently been suggested, his composition was overtaken by the end of the war (which would also explain the *Resonyng*'s non-appearance in published form);[3] or perhaps it was Lamb's death which prevented the writing of the last section.

THE AUTHOR

Although the career of William Lamb has attracted little attention, he was a well-connected courtier and a prominent member of the administration of James V and of Mary of Guise. His multifarious political, academic and ecclesiastical activities, moreover, give us an unusually detailed picture of his life. That he owed much to his family ties is beyond question, for he was the nephew and adopted son of Patrick Paniter (d. 1519), abbot of Cambuskenneth from 1513 until his death and a notably influential royal secretary.[4] In a charter of 10 August 1516, in which Paniter granted various lands belonging to the hospital of St Mary by Montrose to his nephew David, there is a contingent legacy to William Paniter or Lamb, '*nepoti dicti Patricii ex sorore sua, tunc vero filio suo adoptivo*'.[5] Lamb, then, was the son of Paniter's sister, and by 1516 he was established in his uncle's household. For the duration of Patrick Paniter's life, Lamb described himself as 'Paniter *alias* Lamb', a style which he seems to have abandoned as soon as his uncle and patron died. Patrick himself came from a family of some local distinction in Montrose and its vicinity, but which had not hitherto assumed any national significance. By virtue of his outstanding Latinity and, according to his friend Hector Boece, his great skill in political and diplomatic affairs, he became one of the most important of James IV's servants, in a strong position to further the careers of his own illegitimate son, David, and of his sister's son. I have found no suggestion that William Lamb was himself illegitimate, and it seems rather that he could expect little advancement through his father's kin. From the rapidity with which he dropped the Paniter name after Patrick's death, it would seem that he had used it as a mark of his position as *filius adoptivus* rather than as a badge of illegitimacy.[6]

It is clear that Lamb was born in the mid-1490s : when he sought the precentorship of Glasgow in January 1514, his representative at the Papal Court stated that he was in his nineteenth or twentieth year.[7] But six months later, when he was supplicating for the prebend of Conveth, which he was to hold for most of his life, Lamb was stated to be in his twentieth or twenty-first year,[8] from which we can deduce that he had in the meantime celebrated another birthday, but presumably was not sure which. At the earliest, therefore, he cannot have been born before January 1493, while the latest possible date of his birth must be placed in July 1495. At this relatively early age, he became an assiduous seeker of benefices: between 29 December 1513 and 31 October of the following year he supplicated for no fewer than seven such posts, in five separate dioceses as widely separated as Ross, Brechin and Glasgow.[9] These included, as we have already noticed, the precentorship of Glasgow, much too senior a benefice for such a young man to have in normal circumstances any realistic prospect of success.

Only in Conveth, in fact, did Lamb's repeated petitions meet with ultimate success, although he was soon to add the prebend of Croy in the cathedral of Moray and the rectory of Kinnell to that of Conveth.[10] It was as a canon of Moray that he witnessed, on 9 May 1516, the charter by which Patrick Paniter made over some of the lands of the hospital of the Virgin near Montrose for the establishment of a Dominican house in the burgh;[11] but it was more than two months before his supplication to be provided to the prebend of Croy was actually dealt with in Rome. Such a sense of priority was not unusual in sixteenth-century Scotland, but another of Lamb's attempts to extend his ecclesiastical holdings fell foul of a local patron: on 19 February 1517, William earl of Erroll complained to the Lords of Council that William Lamb *alias* Paniter had purchased in Rome a pension of £50 from the rectory of Turriff in the diocese of Aberdeen without his licence, knowledge or consent, 'makand na mentioun that it was ane lawit patronage'. Lamb was represented at this hearing by his uncle, the abbot of Cambuskenneth, whose forensic skills were clearly sufficient to gain a discharge for his nephew.[12] It is not clear whether Lamb ever enjoyed the fruits of Turriff, but on balance it seems unlikely: it was as prebendary of Conveth, Croy and Kinnell (total annual value £70) that he was, by 27 July 1517 and despite the defect of his youth, firmly established.[13]

It is difficult to be certain what training he was receiving during this period. He was already a Master of Arts of another university when he was incorporated at St Andrews in 1520, but there is no record of his attendance anywhere else. He does not appear in the records of Glasgow, Paris, Louvain or Cologne, which had the largest concentrations of Scots at this period,[14] and it is perhaps most likely that, as an Angus man and Patrick Paniter's kinsman and protégé, he made his way to the new University of Aberdeen, where his uncle's Parisian contemporary Hector Boece was Principal. No matriculation or graduation records survive from sixteenth-century Aberdeen, so that we would not expect to find any evidence if this were the case, and it seems probable that the humanist ambiance of King's College would have appealed to Paniter senior.[15] It is also possible that Lamb spent some time in Paris, despite his absence from the University records: Patrick Paniter stayed on there after negotiating the Treaty of Rouen in August 1517, and was still in Paris when he died in the autumn of 1519.[16] Apart from two supplications regarding the church of Inchbrayock near Montrose, which were dealt with in the Papal Court on 26 and 29 December 1517,[17] there was only one approach from Lamb to Rome between August 1517 and November 1519, after the death of Paniter, and that was a correction to a previous provision concerning Conveth, Croy and Kinnell.[18] By comparison with the steady flow of litigation both before and after this period, this interval of a little more than two years is remarkably quiet, and since there are no surviving documents which place Lamb in Scotland in these years, it seems probable that he was in Paniter's household in Paris.

The death of his adopted father appears to have redoubled his pursuit of ecclesiastical preferment, and to have brought him back to Scotland. On his matriculation at St Andrews he is described for the first time as 'Master' as well as rector of Conveth. Although he is nowhere mentioned before this occasion in the generally full records of the University, there does seem to have been some link between Lamb and St Andrews before this time: Kinnell, which he had been seeking as early as July 1517, was a prebend of St Salvator's College, and while Conveth was not formally appropriated (only later becoming a prebend of St Mary's College), it had been held by a number of St Andrews masters, and most recently by David Spens, Rector of the University from 1504 to 1510 and again from 1512 to 1516.[19] At any event, it is clear that Lamb had graduated MA by the time of his arrival in St Andrews in 1520. There was, however, rather more doubt about his clerical status: he is sometimes described as 'clericus aut laicus' in earlier documents,[20] but in November 1519 he was firmly stated to be a layman, and it was confirmed on 20 June 1520 that he was not yet a subdeacon, the first of the three sacred orders.[21] He was, the Papal Court believed, a deacon by 26 April 1521, but he was still not a priest in September of that year, when he was again seeking confirmation of his provision to Croy.[22] He seems, in fact, never to have entered priestly orders at all, and we shall see that his status continued to be a matter of uncertainty for almost another twenty years: there was enough doubt in Rome for him to be described as 'alleged clerk' in a commission of 31 December 1537.[23]

He did, nevertheless, win possession of the three benefices which he had sought so actively, and he now began to establish himself in an academic career at St Andrews, where he appears intermittently in the records over the next few years. He was appointed Visitor of St Salvator's College on 16 January 1522, and acted as assessor that year and again in 1523.[24] He was, moreover, mentioned as a member of the University when its affairs were the subject of an official enquiry in November 1524, although he was listed among those masters who were not continuously resident.[25] One occasion on which he was certainly in St Andrews was for the drawing up of a deed securing the reversion of the lands of Dun from St Salvator's to John Erskine of Dun (16 July 1526), for which he acted as a witness.[26] But his presence could also be in demand elsewhere: on 11 July 1521, in distinguished company, he participated in the rededication of the abbey church at Cambuskenneth and two adjacent cemeteries.[27] Perhaps it was as a result of his connection with the late abbot that Lamb became involved in this ceremony.

It is difficult to build up a coherent picture of Lamb's activities in the 1520s and 1530s. His continuing interest in his native region is reflected in his purchase, on 8 October 1525, of a quarter of the lands of Fullertoun near Montrose from Walter Ogilvie, a burgess of the burgh, a property which he eventually sold, on 24 May 1541, to David Wood of Craig-Inchbriok.[28] But this is his last appearance in the Scottish records for a long time, and we learn from a letter which James V wrote to Benedict, Cardinal-archbishop of Ravenna on 31 March 1531, that he had been living in France 'for some years'.[29] According to James, Lamb was now undertaking a pilgrimage—he does not say where— and the Scottish king hoped that a place would be found for him in the Cardinal's household. This is the only direct evidence that Lamb ever visited Italy, and it is of some importance, therefore, in assessing his cultural environment and the information he may have acquired about humanist historians like Sabellico, a matter to which we shall have to return. It was presumably during this period of residence in France that he commissioned an unusual mark of ownership in some books he purchased: the printer of three works by Jean Fernel, published in 1526 and 1528, has apparently added to each title-page the inscription 'EX LIBRIS M. GVILLERMI LAMBE 1530', and in view of James V's statement it seems certain that Lamb was actually in Paris at this time.[30]

It was no doubt because of his prolonged absence from Scotland that Lamb began to shed his benefices there. Some time before 23 January 1530, he resigned Conveth in favour of Mr Gavin Logie, a St Andrews colleague who was Principal of St Leonard's College, reserving the right of regress should Logie give up the rectory again.[31] It is evident that Lamb was hedging his bets by seeking to retain the right of regress, and on 21 March 1532 he paid the sum of

10 florins 15 shillings towards the annates of Conveth; a strong
family interest in the matter is suggested by the fact that, in
addition to Logie, Lamb's half-brother David Paniter and Patrick
Liddell (described in our manuscript as his brother also) made
similar payments at the same time.[32] This resignation of Conveth
proved the cause of considerable later difficulties. Gavin Logie died
in August 1537, and his rectory was soon the subject of a petition by
James Douglas.[33] Archbishop James Betoun of St Andrews,
however, provided Peter Balfour, Treasurer of Glasgow, and
Lamb was forced to make his own supplication to Pope Paul III in
an attempt to exercise his right of regress.[34] On 10 October 1537,
William Stewart, bishop of Aberdeen, Alexander Myln, abbot of
Cambuskenneth, and James Lyn, canon of Dunkeld, were appointed as Papal commissioners to deal with the dispute.[35] Not
only Conveth was involved in the contest, for two years later Lamb
and Balfour were still at odds over the payment of £100 from the
fruits of Logie-Montrose, a benefice for which Lamb had first
supplicated at the end of 1513 but which then disappears for nearly
twenty-five years from his life-story.[36] That he had ultimately
succeeded in obtaining the rectory of Logie-Montrose would
appear from the fact that he was seeking a new provision in
October 1537, along with Croy and Moy, Kinnell and Conveth,
apparently doubtful about the legitimacy of his existing claims.[37]
Presumably, he had subsequently resigned Logie-Montrose as
well: we know that he had given up Croy and Moy in favour of
Patrick Liddell at some date before 25 September 1534.[38]

Whether or not Lamb was back in Scotland by the time he
began to re-assert his claims in the autumn of 1537—and it would
seem most likely that he was—he had certainly returned before 4
February 1538, when he was appointed by James V to the number
of the Lords of Council.[39] He was, moreover, described in the
king's letter as rector of Conveth, indicating that he had succeeded
in his attempts to regain the benefice, at least in the eyes of the
government. Lamb now began to play a significant part in royal
administration, building perhaps on his Continental experience.
He was a full member of the royal council by 27 January 1540, and
now turns up as one of the distinguished judges of the College of

Justice, the new superior court which had been established by James V in 1532 and which included among its number Alexander Myln as President, Henry Sinclair, rector of Glasgow and subsequently bishop of Ross and President of the College, John Sinclair, rector of Restalrig, and the Reformer Henry Balnavis.[40] His responsibilities were now both judicial and political, and like other experienced administrators he must have played a crucial role in government when the outbreak of war with England in 1542 was quickly followed by the disaster of Solway Moss and the death of the king. The politics of the minority of Queen Mary were complicated in the extreme, as Cardinal Betoun, the Queen Mother Mary of Guise, the earls of Arran and Argyll and other magnates contended for control.[41] The role of professional administrators like Lamb must have been of great importance in the everyday running of government, but only twice in these troubled years, on 21 October 1544 and in June 1545, do we find concrete evidence, in the form of entries in the Treasurer's Accounts recording payments for the writing of letters to Lamb among other prominent councillors.[42] Although sederunt lists for the Council do not generally survive during this period, it seems probable that he was a regular participant in its affairs.

Curiously enough, it is only financial disputes which give us a few glimpses of his involvements during the minority of Mary. On 27 November 1546, he was one of the Senators of the College of Justice who refused to pay the taxes which had been levied to pay for the siege of St Andrews castle after the assassination of Cardinal Betoun, claiming that the privileges of their office included exemption from such duties, a protest which was eventually accepted by the Council on 19 March 1548.[43] It would seem that in this instance personal interest prevailed over political conviction, since the pro-Catholic and anti-English tone of the *Resonyng* surely indicate that Lamb's sympathies would have been with the objectives of the besiegers. In any event, a more serious financial problem was the stipend to which the Senators were entitled, the non-payment of which was a burning issue throughout the 1540s. When a sum of £3,000 was ultimately made available for distribution, the matter having come to a head in February 1550,

Lamb was owed—and now received—nine years' back salary at
£40 per annum.[44]

Within a few months of this settlement, Lamb was dead. On 21
September 1550, Mr Patrick Liddell, canon of Moray and
prebendary of Croy and Moy, was supplicating for provision to
Conveth, Logie-Montrose and Kinnell, all vacant by the death of
William Lamb.[45] His difficulties were to prove even greater than
those which Lamb himself had experienced thirteen years earlier.
Kinnell was apparently obtained by David Paniter, although
Liddell would make another attempt when Paniter resigned the
benefice in March 1553.[46] His opponent in Logie-Montrose was
Alexander Forrest, and again Liddell was unsuccessful.[47] Conveth
eventually became linked with St Mary's College when it was
established in 1554.[48] Lamb died, as far as we can tell, without
heirs, and his name passed into oblivion, despite his clear
importance in the Scottish administration of the 1540s. All he
would appear to have left behind was a literary curiosity, which
has until now lain almost unnoticed in manuscript.

DATE AND OCCASION

The approximate date of the *Resonyng* can fairly easily be fixed
on the basis of internal evidence. From a reference to 'þir sevin
ʒeiris [of] iust weir' (7/1), it follows that Lamb's dialogue could
scarcely have been composed before 1549—and by Lamb's own
data the statement would only be strictly true after July of that
year—while the fact that Somerset is apparently still regarded as
Protector indicates that it must have preceded his fall in October,
or news of it reaching Scotland. Other details suggest that it was
begun well before the autumn: the Inglis Merchand's opening
boast that the English 'dois baith ruffill ʒow and þe Frenchemen'
(3/15-5/1) would have seemed increasingly empty as 1549 pro-
gressed, and whereas d'Esse's French forces had failed to take
Haddington in the latter part of the previous year the English,
their supply lines overstretched and their strength quickly dissipat-
ing, were forced by mid-September 1549 to abandon their last
remaining strongholds, Haddington and Broughty Castle.[49] More

generally, the underlying argument of the *Resonyng* clearly supposes that the war is continuing in full spate, so that its origins must precede the first signs of the English collapse. The balance of probabilities, therefore, is that Lamb began work on his dialogue in the spring or early summer of 1549, when the reference to seven years of war was approximately right, and that it was left in its present incomplete form when the war was manifestly entering its final stages, just before the fall of Somerset.[50]

Such exact information about the date of the tract enables us to be fairly precise also about its circumstances. In the course of 1547–48, the Scots had been subjected to an unprecedented barrage of printed propaganda, no fewer than five works aimed at establishing the ancient superiority of England over Scotland and/or the desirability of a union in which England would quite clearly be the leading partner, appearing in the course of these two years.[51] The only Scottish response which has hitherto been noted is *The Complaynt of Scotland*, an anonymous work which is attributed, with some credibility but with less than complete certainty, to Robert Wedderburn.[52] Whoever the author was, it is evident from the terms of his dedicatory epistle to Mary of Guise, and indeed from the whole cast of his work, that he was like Lamb a courtier close to the centre of Scottish political life. This dedicatory letter was composed after the young Queen Mary's departure for France (August 1548) and before Mary of Guise joined her daughter there (September 1550), since the author alludes to

ʒour grace beand absent fra only ʒong dochter, our nobil princes and rychteous heretour of scotland, quha is presentlye veil tretit in the gouernance of hir fadir of lau . . .[53]

The *Complaynt*'s most recent editor believes that the work was commenced in 1549 and published, with some modifications to take account of the changing political circumstances, in the first half of the following year.[54] The first stage of composition would, according to this very convincing argument, then be contemporary with Lamb's writing of the *Resonyng*; and the fact that Lamb's work was left incomplete, and apparently never published, would be due to the same cause as explains the revisions to *The Complaynt of Scotland*, namely that the English effort to subdue Scotland had collapsed in the summer and autumn of 1549.

The Complaynt of Scotland and Lamb's *Resonyng*, we may surely conclude, were initiated together, by authors who knew each other and who existed in the same milieu, as parallel responses to Somerset's propaganda campaign. There is, moreover, some evidence of influence or collusion in the two works. Both writers employ a distinctive proverbial metaphor, the burning of a father's stick of chastisement, in identical contexts (*Resonyng*, 5/4; *Complaynt*, ed. Stewart, p. 22), and both play with the Platonic notion of the transmigration of souls (*Resonyng*, 171/7; *Complaynt*, ed. Stewart, p. 26). Such parallels are unlikely, given the nature of the other evidence, to be coincidental, and we must conclude either that one had read the work of the other or that the two men, both quite probably amateur authors, discussed their work as it proceeded. From the differences in their respective versions of Platonic metempsychosis (neither of which is strictly accurate), it seems more probable that the parallels are the result of discussion than that one author had read the work of the other; but the position of the references to Plato at the beginning of the *Complaynt* and in the final paragraph of the *Resonyng* suggests that if one man did borrow from the other, it was Lamb who was the borrower.[55]

SOURCES

The most obvious and fundamental source of the *Resonyng*, and its *raison d'etre*, is the work to which it replies, *A Declaration, contenyning the ivst cavses and consyderations, of this present warre with the Scottis, wherin alsoo appereth the trewe & right title, that the kinges most royall maiesty hath to the souerayntie of Scotlande*, prepared by the English government and printed by Thomas Berthelet in 1542.[56] Its arguments provide the framework of Lamb's dialogue, and indeed they are the very fabric of the English merchant's speeches almost throughout the discussion (from 21/13 in the present edition). Lamb has simply taken each successive claim which is made in the *Declaration* and put it into the mouth of his English character, in most cases without any substantive alteration. The propaganda advantage of this technique is clear enough: the English arguments are presented unadorned and unaltered, so that there can be no suggestion that the Scottish merchant's refutations do not respond to the claims made by the opposition. But it cannot be said that the result is a lively interchange of ideas, for Lamb's methods never give the English merchant an opportunity to respond to his Scottish companion's case. Nor is there any evidence that Lamb made any attempt to look behind the *Declaration* at the sources of the English treatise, which very probably included the list of alleged Scottish homages compiled by the English chronicler and forger John Hardyng in the middle of the fifteenth century.[57]

For the first part of the debate, that which deals with Anglo-Scottish relations from about 1500 until the outbreak of war in 1542, Lamb relies upon primary materials in constructing his answers to the English allegations of bad Scottish faith. Although a few of his details appear to be inaccurate, and his chronology is sometimes a little confused, there can be no doubt that his account of this period is highly circumstantial and in many respects well-informed. It was, of course, his own lifetime: he was a small child when Sir Robert Kerr of Ferniehurst was murdered a little before 1500 (23/1), and was already teaching at St Andrews during the border war of 1522–23. Some of his account, therefore, may be based upon his own recollection, and the apparent confusion of events in the 1520s with the subsequent campaigns of 1532–33 may have something to do with the fact that he was probably out of the country during the latter period. But Lamb does not rely entirely upon his own memory, and this first stage of the argument is plentifully supplied with references to 'sindre writtingis of Kyng Henry the Aucht' (27/7), 'þe Greitt Seill of Ingland in our Registre' (33/17), and the like. Two points emerge from this approach to documentation. In the first place, Lamb's preoccupation with 'pruif' (which he also calls 'probatioun') is fundamental to the structure of his argument: the *Resonyng* is a lawyer's work, with a lawyer's attention to evidence. This is, indeed, Lamb's greatest strength as an historian, and if his judgment is not always impeccable, and his enthusiasm for his brief sometimes leads him into excessive claims, nevertheless he is careful about his documentation. Any historian is, of course, only as good as his sources, and this leads to the second point: that Lamb, an active member of the Scottish government, tried to make the most of his access to the official archives. His references to 'our Registre' reveal his familiarity with the original diplomatic documents, and he tellingly employs the texts of the so-called Treaty of Northampton of 1328, the originals of which he would appear to have seen, to climax his refutation of the English case.[58]

When he moved on to the second part of the *Declaration*, that listing the purported homages of Scottish kings from the time of Constantine II and of Athelstan of England in the tenth century to that of James I, Lamb was faced with a more serious problem of documentation. Some of these events were probably invented, and therefore hardly susceptible to proof, while concerning others Lamb probably had no access to documentary evidence. His response was a simple one, but nevertheless inspired: to take as his principal source the history of England which had been published by the Italian humanist Polydore Vergil in 1534. 'ȝour Polidor' is Lamb's trump card, for his account differs in very many particulars from that of the *Declaration*, and he is scarcely a witness who can be charged by the English with pro-Scottish bias. His statements thus become the foundation of many of the Scottish merchant's most effective replies, and long quotations in the original Latin are included (with small attention to dramatic verisimilitude) on numerous occasions. Again, Lamb emerges as a careful and critical reader of his source-material, and if he is over-reliant on the accuracy of Polydore Vergil's account, and his chronological calculations are sometimes difficult to follow, he is much closer to the truth at several points than his English opponents.

By the time Lamb was writing his *Resonyng* in 1549, two editions of the *Anglica Historia* had appeared, the first in 1534, the second in 1546. Although the text is for the most part not materially different, and there seems to be nothing to justify Lamb's claim that the English government forced Polydore Vergil into some kind of recantation (67/7), there are numerous small variants, a few of which occur in passages quoted by Lamb.[59] The Scottish author himself refers to 'þe first prent' of the *Anglica Historia*, and comparison of the two editions with Lamb's text leaves no doubt that it was the 1534 edition which he had in front of him as he worked. We can, it is true, attach small importance to the fact that at 95/5 he follows the 1534 text in referring to the Scottish king 'Macolmus' where the 1546 version reads 'Malcolmus', but it is more revealing that at 103/2 he includes the word 'quippe' in a passage from which it was accidentally omitted in 1546. He could, in other words, have found his correct version only in the 1534 edition. The conclusive reading is at 115/14, in the phrase 'sed dominum Scotie ageret' (the MS. of the *Resonyng* here reads 'ageretis', but cf. the correct reading when the passage is repeated at 145/26): 'ageret' comes from the 1534 edition, and was replaced in 1546 with 'præberet'. The issue therefore seems to be settled beyond question: Lamb drew his quotations and his arguments from the earlier edition of the *Anglica Historia*.

In addition to Polydore Vergil, Lamb makes occasional use of other humanist historians. Although he seems reluctant, perhaps for tactical reasons, to rely much on Scottish sources, he does make three references to the *Scotorum Historiæ* (1527) of Hector Boece, whom he dignifies with the title of 'our trew historiciane' (57/9). While Boece, whose work reveals that penchant for implausible myth and rhetorical excess which is so characteristic of some humanist historians and so alien to Lamb's approach, scarcely justifies Lamb's compliment, the *Resonyng* shows that its author had made a careful comparison of his sources, and the restrained use which he makes of Boece—indicating, for example, that he differs from Polydore Vergil in the name he assigns to the daughter of the Saxon king Edward—does his case no harm. Boece's French counterpart, the Trinitarian Robert Gaguin, whose *De Francorum gestis* (1507) was the first attempt at a comprehensive humanist history of France, is also invoked once, *a propos* the date of the marriage between Henry II of England and Eleanor of Aquitaine (97/26). More interestingly, perhaps, Lamb dismisses the English treatise's use of a statement by the Venetian historian Sabellico (Marcantonio Coccio) not only on the grounds that the statement itself is absurd, but also that Sabellico:

as can be provin hes errit baith in historie and discriptioun of landis
about his awin durris in Italie.   (65/17–19)

This rather jaundiced view contrasts sharply with the high regard
in which Sabellico was apparently held by Italian historians for
most of the sixteenth-century, although his credulous acceptance
of legends, especially those which helped to glorify Venice, was
criticised by a later generation, and his analysis of the Venetian
constitution had already received some criticism in Donato
Gianotti's *Della Repubblica de' Veneziani*, published in Rome in
1540.[60] Lamb is not specific in his allegations of inaccuracy, but it
may be that he was relying on information he had acquired during
the visit which he apparently made to Italy in 1531.

Constrained as he allows himself to be by the structure of the
English *Declaration*, Lamb never develops his historical arguments
very far. The most discriminating use of source-material which he
offers is in his demolition of the English claim to superiority
deriving from the supposed division of Britain among the three sons
of the mythical Brutus, but the truth is that Lamb can take little
credit for this example of historical criticism: his three authorities,
Caesar, Tacitus and Gildas, are all invoked in the same terms and
in the same order by Polydore Vergil near the beginning of the
Anglica Historia.[61] Even so, by choosing to follow Polydore and thus
avoiding the counter-mythologising of his Scottish predecessors,
who sought to deal with the English claims by inventing and
perpetuating their own, equally fictitious genealogy for the
Scottish 'race'.[62] Lamb reveals a measure of discrimination.
Again, his forensic approach to evidence may be standing him in
good stead, and while his careful setting of contradictory statements side by side may not make exciting reading, it constitutes an
effective answer to the more extravagent of the English arguments.

Lamb's firm dependence on a very limited range of historical
sources, decorated only by the occasional maxim or Classical
allusion and some rather pawky rhetorical thrusts, contrasts
strikingly with the approach adopted by the author of *The
Complaynt of Scotland*. His principal source, after all, is neither an
English propaganda-tract nor any historical work, but a vigorous

French dialogue, Alain Chartier's *Quadrilogue invectif*.[63] Even if we do not take into account the rhetorical pyrotechnics of the 'Monologue Recreative', which would seem to have been added while the *Complaynt* was already in type, there is no doubt that the *Complaynt* is stylistically more varied and all in all a much more *literary* work than Lamb's *Resonyng*. When rhetorical figures and literary allusions are occasionally allowed to creep into the *Resonyng*, they are there merely to spice the argument or to clinch a point, and Lamb's style is consistently more severe than that of his fellow-propagandist. Consideration of the sources, like every other dimension of the *Resonyng*, reveals Lamb as a resourceful advocate and a sensible historian by the standards of his day, but as a man with a limited interest in the demands of aesthetics.

THE DIALOGUE FORM

In choosing to cast his work in the form of a dialogue Lamb set up, as we have seen, a pattern in which he could restate the English case and then seek to demolish its elements one by one. But he was also conforming to a current vogue, for the value of the dialogue in political and doctrinal controversy was not lost upon his contemporaries. Lamb may not have been aware of the rash of Protestant works in dialogue form which had appeared during the previous couple of years—such as William Turner's *New Dialogue* (1548), *A Dialogue bytwene a gentylman and a prest* (1547), *John Bon and Mest Parson* (*c*.1548), and Punt's *Endyghtment against Mother Messe* (1549)[64]—but the application of the form to such purposes was not in itself new, and it is likely that he had come across one or more works in the genre.

It is possible to identify at least three separate strands in the development of the mid-sixteenth century dialogue. One is the Socratic form, the rhetorical use of discussion in the analysis of philosophical questions which has its origins in the works of Plato and which had also been adopted in antiquity by Lucian. It was taken up with some enthusiasm by humanist writers, both in the guise of translations such as the Latin version of Lucian produced by Thomas More, and in original works such as the enormously influential *Colloquia* of Erasmus. The latter had themselves begun to be translated into the vernacular by Lamb's day: the first of the *Colloquia* to be published in English appeared about 1540, and *The epicure* was printed in 1545. A similar application of the dialogue to the exposition of ideas, though with a more popular emphasis, can be found in a few works like *Of Gentylnes and Nobylyte* (printed c.1535), deriving from an Italian model: the *Controversia de nobilitate* of Buonaccorso was translated by John Tiptoft and printed by Caxton as early as 1481.[65]

All these works are in prose, but a parallel development descending from antiquity, which may in some formal respect have influenced the controversial dialogue, was that of the eclogue. Virgil's eclogues are, of course, cast in dialogue form, and his example was followed by all his humanist imitators: Petrarch, Boccaccio and, most significantly for the vernacular tradition, Mantuan. It was Mantuan's pastoral poems which were imitated and in part translated by Alexander Barclay, who incorporated into his five *Egloges* (which were printed, separately or together, in several editions in the first half of the century) some discussion of such well-established moral themes as the miserable life of courtiers.[66]

But the most significant strand of the dialogue tradition for an understanding of Lamb, and the one which accounts for the vogue for controversial dialogues in the later 1540s, is that which seems to begin with the anti-Catholic tracts of such Lutheran writers as Hans Sachs. This tradition was itself a distant cousin of the Socratic dialogue, but its atmosphere was altogether different and its objectives much more precise. Rather than exploring philosophical doctrines in a scholarly manner, Lutheran authors were engaged in a vigorous form of religious controversy, and this is clearly manifested in such early English examples as *Rede me and be not wrothe*, attributed to William Roy and Jerome Barlow and published in Strasbourg in 1529.[67] In such cases, there is even less interest in contrasts of character or the interplay of ideas than is apparent in the humanist colloquy or the pastoral eclogue, and all the emphasis falls upon the exposition of dogma and the demolition of opposing points of view. The characters are generally stereotyped, so that the rhetorical mainspring is the opposition of Catholic priest and honest, Reforming layman (a Scottish adaptation of this scenario can be found in Sir David Lyndsay's *Testament and Complaynt of the Papyngo*, written in 1530), two representative social types, as in *The gentillman and a husbandman* (1530), or even between allegorical characters (*A Dialogue betweene knowledge and symplicitie*, an undated edition of which is among the English tracts which are roughly contemporary with Lamb's *Resonyng*).[68]

It is obviously impossible to judge which, if any, of these various works Lamb might have read; but there are some clear affinities between the *Resonyng* and the contemporary English dialogues. His interest in the rhetorical possibilities of the form is, as we have seen, quite limited, and it is the lawyer's approach to debate which seems to dominate the construction of the work. In the main sections of the discussion, there is seldom any real interchange between the protagonists: the English merchant makes a claim (almost invariably a short quotation from the 1542 *Declaration*), the Scottish merchant refutes it at some length, sometimes simply marshalling the contrary evidence, sometimes engaging in a rhetorical jibe as well, and the English merchant moves on to the next point without attempting any rebuttal. This simple and rather unimaginative pattern is perhaps intended to suggest that the Scottish merchant's arguments are unanswerable; or it may be, as suggested above, that Lamb was determined to let the *Declaration* stand or fall purely on its own terms. The English merchant is given an occasional rhetorical thrust:

ʒow Scottis be to laith for to knawlege ʒour errour (95/20–21).
Giff I will say þe craw is blak, than ʒow will say þat scho is quhytt? (133/1–2).

But for the most part Lamb is an astute enough rhetorician to give such enlivening remarks to the Scot, who has the best lines as well as the sounder arguments.

The fictional occasion of the dialogue appears to have preoccupied Lamb little more than the interaction of his characters or the development of the characters themselves. The title announces that the two merchants are travelling 'betuix Rowand and Lyonis &c.', and it seems that all the characters have a common destination in the great trading city of Lyon. The only use which is subsequently made of this rather promising situation, however, is as a basis of structural division: the end of that part of the discussion which deals with the recent history of Anglo-Scottish relations is marked by the arrival of the party in Rouen (53/27), but Lamb is so cavalier in his treatment of his central fictive device that Rouen again appears after the long debate about the homages of Scottish kings (129/23). Unless the merchants have been proceeding in a huge circle, we must surely conclude that Lamb was insufficiently engaged with his fiction to iron out such an obvious inconsistency! By the time that the last section of the *Declaration* has been disposed of, at the end of the completed portion of the *Resonyng*, the travellers are approaching Paris. This leaves, of course, a great deal of the announced journey to be completed, and it was presumably Lamb's original intention to devote this remaining section to the countering of the Protector Somerset's *Exhortàtioun*, the 'vthir buik' of the *Resonyng*'s final phrase. Apart from these token references, which differentiate the main sections of the argument, the motif of the journey scarcely enters into the reader's consciousness.

Frustratingly, the same sense of a good idea wasted applies even more strongly to the introduction of the three mysterious horsemen whom the merchants encounter at 9/15. We quickly discover that they are Thomas More, John Fisher and the 'Guid Man of Sion'; and though neither they nor the merchants comment upon the fact, we are clearly expected to register that they are all victims of Henry VIII's ecclesiastical repression. Such a startling breach of verisimilitude, brought into the narrative with so little fuss, has many dramatic and doctrinal possibilities, but apart from some rather puzzling play with the subject of transmigration of souls at the conclusion of the *Resonyng*, about which we shall have to say a little more in a moment, Lamb virtually ignores the surrealistic situation he has created. The Guid Man of Sion, who is never identified further but who was in fact the Brigittine Richard Reynolds, does allude to a time 'quhen I duelt in Ingland' (13/12)—a phrase with clear ironic significance in the circumstances—but his role in the dialogue is really as no more than an impartial arbiter, to whom the merchants, and particularly the Scot, appeal from time to time. There may, too, be a wry note in More's observation that 'We merchandis makis small game in tyme of weir!' (15/5); but there is no real reason to suppose that Lamb was aware of More's mercantile background. Neither More nor Fisher makes any further contribution to the discussion after this point, and for most of the way the Guid Man's comments are confined to the occasional geographical marker noted above.

Only at the very end does Lamb attempt a more adventurous ploy in his fiction. Responding to the Scottish merchant's peroration, the Guid Man acknowledges the force of many of his arguments, undertakes to form a firmer judgement after reading Polydore Vergil, and denies any pro-English prejudice. He then harks back to the days of his residence in England:

Quhen I did hant in Ingland, þair regnit ane nobill prince, Kyng Henrie þe viij., quhais naturale guidnes wes oftymes alterat be counsell. Also þan þe new leirnyng of Germanie entiris in his court—quhat, be þis kyng deith?   (169/15–20).

It really is extraordinary that Lamb should make Reynolds speak in these terms of the man responsible for his execution, but the improbability of his sentiments would appear to be an important part of the point. It is also notable that the Guid Man is used by Lamb to shift some of the blame away from Henry VIII and towards his advisers: the dependence of political order upon good advice is a truism of medieval theory. But curious as this brief apologia for Henry may seem in the context, it is relatively straightforward by comparison with the Guid Man's following remarks. Informed by the English Merchant that the king is indeed dead, he first laments the extension of 'þe new leirnyng' which he believes will now be unleashed (a pointed reference to the growth of a more overtly Protestant emphasis in the English Reformation in the reign of Edward VI), and then speculates that the fashion for radical thinking may bring about a revival of certain doctrines of 'þe auld philosophouris'. This makes him even more reluctant to support the Scottish merchant's case, he says, since if Plato was right the whole cycle of history might repeat itself after 48,000 years. This is a cumbersome joke, but Lamb is trying to make a satritical point about the vigour of English persecution of dissenters, which causes the Guid Man to take the most extreme precautions. It is a pity that the unfinished state of the *Resonyng* denies us the further discussion of Platonic and Pythagorean doctrines of reincarnation which the Guid Man promises us.

LANGUAGE

The language of the *Resonyng* as it is preserved in MS. Cotton Caligula B.vii is fairly typical of Scots texts of the mid-sixteenth century. The best systematic discussion of Older Scots are those by CH Kuipers[69] and CC van Buuren-Veenenbos,[70] and it is unnecessary to repeat in what follows the basic structure defined by them. The following list of features is therefore an attempt to identify the more important and distinctive characteristics of the grammar and orthography of the *Resonyng*, given that in most respects the practice of the scribe does not differ materially from the usage found by Fr Kuipers in the manuscripts of Quintin Kennedy's tracts.

(i) *Nouns*: The inflection of nouns in both the possessive and the plural is normally -*is*, although the form *historijs* occurs as well as *historiis* and (once) *historyis*. There are a number of other exceptions:

Possessive: *uncles*, 33/12; *heretrice*, 9/1; *þe deid selfe*, 17/3, 45/17; *Edward þe Secund selfe*, 105/4.

Plural: *realmes*, 125/1; *tymes*, 167/16; *childring*, 5/5, 63/4, 113/5; *brethering*, 59/9. (Although the number of instances is small, -*ing* appears to be the scribe's usual way of spelling the -*en* inflection: the mutation form *brethir* occurs as guid-brethir, 91/10.

(ii) *Adjectives*: Plural adjectives are not usually inflected, but there are a few instances of agreement:

þe saidis twa buikis, 9/6; *nobillis fugitivis*, 31/26–27, 33/8; *forsaidis homagis*, 119/12–13; *excusatorijs writtingis*, 25/8. The post-posed adjective, another manifestation of French influence on M.Sc. style, is even less a feature of Lamb's usage, but there is one example: *ane guid sentence diffinitiue*, 19/6–7.

(iii) *Comparatives and Superlatives*: The forms in both adjectives and adverbs are consistently *-ar* and *-ast*:
hear, weichtear, 13/17; *langar*, 51/28, 159/28; ʒongar, 59/8; *greitar*, 119/20; *fastar*, 155/27 (but cf. *þe nerther*, 155/25); *wysast*, 17/20; *nerrast*, 27/15, 69/25, 89/19; *abillast*, 89/19.

(iv) *Verbs*: In the present indicative of verbs, the normal pattern of inflection is:

	Sing.	Plural
1	—	—
2	*-is*	—
3	*-is*	—

Occasionally, forms other than 2nd and 3rd person sing. are given an *-is* inflection: this may reflect the common M.Sc. practice of inflecting the second of two verbs sharing a single subject (*we reid and findis*, 89/4; *þe quhilk I hald and clames*, 135/16), but plural verbs are also sometimes inflected when they occur alone: *we makis*, 15/5; *we knawis*, 69/9; *þe Inglis courtisiants nedis*, 163/13–14; *þe Scottis hes*, 163/16. The forms of the present indicative of the verb *be* which are found in the *Resonyng* are:

	Sing.	Plural
1	*am*	*be*
2	*be*	*ar*
3	*is/beis*	*be/ar/is*

The inflection of the present participle is normally-*and*; forms of the past participle include (for weak verbs) *-it*, and for strong verbs *-in* (occasionally *-ing*, especially in the case of *cuming*) or the various types of vowel-mutation.

(v) *Relative Pronouns*:

Nom.	*quha*	*quhilk* (pl. *quhilkis*)
Obj.	*quham*	*quhilk*
	quhom(e)	

Poss.   *quhais*   [*of þe quhilkis*]
          quhayis

As the above details suggest, the Cotton manuscript of the *Resonyng* is written throughout in a fairly consistent form of later Middle Scots. One feature, however, is the occurrence of many words in two (sometimes three) different forms. Sometimes, these indicate alternative sources of a loan-word, as in the pair *pruif* (from OF. *preuve*) and *probatioun* (more directly derived from Lat. *probatio*); Lamb uses the two words interchangeably, not making any obvious semantic distinction between them. Similarly, the pair *appunct* and *apoynt*, with their derivatives *disappunct* and *disapoynt* (*disapoynting*, etc.), are borrowed from Lat. and OF. respectively.[71] Both these forms had been current in M.Sc. since the first half of the fifteenth century, but it is striking that Lamb's repertoire includes both. Another such case is the pair *nepot/nephieu*. Such diversity was, of course, a feature of M.Sc., and indeed of Middle English, but the *Resonyng* reflects to the full the wide range of possibilities, in prepositions, adverbs and conjunctions as well as in the more substantive cases just identified. Thus, Lamb variously employs *befoir*, *afoir* and *or*; *betuix* and *betuene*; *quhill*, *till* and *vntill*; and *sa*, *swa* and *so*. For the most part, these alternatives should not perhaps be regarded as representing 'Scots' and 'anglicized' options: *betuix* and *betuene*, to take a particularly clear example, are both attested in a variety of contexts from the fourteenth century on, and neither can properly be identified as resulting from English influence.[72]

The consistency of Lamb's Scots is, indeed, the *Resonyng*'s most distinctive linguistic feature. This observation applies even to those passages which are taken directly from the *Declaration*, where the logic of verisimilitude might have suggested that the English merchant should be allowed to speak in English. Neither in the passages of dialogue based upon the arguments of the *Declaration*, however, nor in the other sections of the *Resonyng* does Lamb ever attempt to distinguish between the usages of his characters, and a comparison between the text of the *Declaration* and that of *Resonyng* illustrates some interesting linguistic points. For example:

Declaration	*Resonyng*
It hath ben very rarely and seldom seen before, that a king of Scottis hath had in mariage a doughter of Englande . . .	. . . for saldin wes it sene befoir þat ane Scottis kyng had in mariage a dochtir of Ingland. (33/22–4)

Apart from the obvious orthographic features (*ane* for *a*, the Scottish scribe's preference for *þ*, the introduction of the familiar Scots forms *befoir* and *dochtir*), Lamb has recast the sentence, partly perhaps to give it greater rhetorical sharpness, but in the process eliminating the two constructions in *hath*, which would seem less natural in Scots than they do in English. The Scots form *saldin* has also been introduced for English *seldom*; three lines further on Lamb uses the even more markedly Scottish *sindlare* (35/1).

A rather more extended passage reveals the same process of adaptation:

Declaration	*Resonyng*
. . . the lorde Maxwell, warden of the west marches of Scotland, made proclamation for good rule, but yet added therwith, that the bourderers of Scotlande shuld withdrawe their goodes from the bourders of Englande: And incontinentely after the Scottishe men bourdurers, the fourth of July, entred into our realme sodeynly, and spoyled our subiectes, contrary to our leages, euen after suche extremitie, as it had bene in tyme of open warre. Whereat we moche maruailed, and were compelled therfore to furnische our bourdour with a garrison for defence of the same.	. . . and siclik Lord Maxwell, Warden of þe Scottis West Merchis, did proclame guid ordour; bot he addit in his proclamatioun that the bordouraris of Scotland suld withdraw þair guidis from the bordouris of Ingland, and incontinent þaireftir þe Scottis bordouraris enterit in Ingland, spuilȝeit our subiectis *a contra* þe leagis maid betuix the kyngis, quharat Kyng Henry merualit mekill and wes compellit þairfore to furneiss þe Inglis bordouraris with a garnesoun of defence. (47/21–49/8)

Again, the superficial changes in spelling practice are sufficient to give the text of the *Resonyng* a clear Scottish cast, but Lamb's use of his original goes further than mere re-spelling. The introduction of the legal term *spuilʒeit* (along with Lamb's favourite *a contra*) gives precision to the English merchant's charge, and the elimination of some of the detail from the *Declaration* account again heightens the rhetorical argument. More important for the present discussion, however, are the representation of *whereat we moche maruailed* by *quharat Kyng Henry merualit mekill*, where the transposition of verb and adverb plays its part in giving an idiomatic flavour to the Scots phrase. In addition to being a skilful editor of his materials, therefore, Lamb has a definite ear for the cadences of Scottish speech, and he maintains the Scots element without distinction of character.

It would be absurd to suggest that Lamb's *Resonyng*, neglected for so long, is a major new literary work. Its historical importance is considerable: it enables us to read the *Complaynt of Scotland* more clearly in its context, and it gives us an insight into the propaganda battle which accompanied the later stages of the Anglo-Scottish war of 1542–49. It also gives, in a fair degree of detail, a well-informed Scotsman's view of the events of the previous half-century, conditioned of course by his desire to make the best of the Scottish case and to condemn the English. But its intrinsic interest goes beyond these historical points. The *Resonyng* is the earliest surviving prose dialogue in Scots, written by a man who was skilled in forensic rhetoric and who had a manifest awareness of the possibilities and limitations of historical evidence. As an exercise in historical argument it is much more serious than the *Complaynt*, and although its focus is always limited by the particularity of Lamb's preoccupations, its flashes of pawky humour and its severe rhetorical style have their attractions. Lamb was capable of literary conceptions with wonderful potential—most obviously, in his introduction of three ghostly horsemen—but failure of imagination or an excessively legalistic superego prevented him from making full use of them. At the very least, however, he deserves credit for approximating the praise he confers, with dubious critical judgment, on Hector Boece: 'our awin trew historiciane'.

THE PRESENT EDITION

On the right-hand pages, I have presented as accurate a text as possible from the only extant manuscript of Lamb's *Resonyng*. The spelling system of the MS. is retained, but punctuation and capitalization have been modernized. In particular, *u/v/w* and *i/j* have been retained; the character *v* is represented as *y* or *þ* according to the context (the fact that Scottish scribes did not distinguish between these letters never in practice creates an ambiguity). Initial *ff* has been regarded as a form of capital letter, and modernized accordingly. Abbreviations and suspensions have been expanded in conformity with the normal practice of the scribe elsewhere in the MS., and indicated in the edition by underlining.

Opposite the text, the Commentary includes, as well as historical and other explanatory notes, the passages which Lamb quotes from the 1542 *Declaration* and the 1534 edition of Polydore Vergil's *Anglica Historia*. These have been presented as they appear in the originals, except that abbreviations have been silently expanded. The purpose here has been to provide the reader with evidence of Lamb's editorial practice, and to permit direct comparison of the original and the quotation. References are to the original texts; in the case of the *Declaration*, this is supplemented by a page-reference to the text presented by JAH Murray in his edition of *The Complaynt of Scotland*. There are a number of blank left hand pages where the text did not appear to require elucidation.

NOTES

[1] Sir Robert Cotton (1571–1631) was the outstanding collector of the latter part of the reign of Elizabeth I and in that of James I, to the extent that the government became concerned about his accummulation of state papers, including some bequeathed to him by Arthur Agard, keeper of the public records; see the fairly full account in *DNB*.

[2] Strictly speaking, the moment for publication was before the collapse of the English campaign in Scotland in mid-September 1549 and the fall of the Protector Somerset three weeks later: see below, pp. xvii–xix.

[3] See Marcus Merriman, 'War and Propaganda during the "Rough Wooing"', *Scottish Tradition* 9/10 (1979–80), 20–30, at 27.

[4] On the life of Patrick Paniter, see the account in the Introduction to *The Letters of James IV*, ed. R. K. Hannay and R. L. Mackie (SHS, Edinburgh 1953), pp. xxviii–xxxiv.

[5] *RMS*, iii, no. 3086.

[6] Lamb is consistently identified as William Paniter, or William Paniter alias Lamb until the autumn of 1519, and thereafter always as William Lamb.

[7] Vatican Archives, Reg. Supp., 1441, ff. 283^{v}–284^{r}.

[8] *ibid.*, 1477, 268^{r-v}.

[9] *ibid.*, 1427, 162^{v}–164^{r}; 1457, 245^{v}; 1462, 49^{r-v}; 1479, 180^{r-v}; 1477, 268^{r-v}.

[10] All three were confirmed to Lamb in the summer of 1517, *ibid.*, 1581, 77^{v}; 1583, 146^{r-v}.

[11] *RMS*, iii, no. 113.

[12] The case is recorded in the *Acts of the Lords of Council in Public Affairs* 1501–54, ed. R. K. Hannay (Edinburgh 1932), p. 77.

[13] Reg. Supp., 1581, 77^{v}.

[14] The records of Glasgow, which include graduation lists in Arts, are printed in *Munimenta Universitatis Glasguensis*, ed. C. Innes (Bannatyne Club, 3 vols, Glasgow 1854); the matriculation albums of Cologne and Louvain for this period have also been published, in editions by H. Keussen and E. Reusens and others respectively. Records of graduations at Paris, which exist for the early sixteenth century, have not yet been edited, but I am informed by Dr John Durkan that Lamb's name is not found there.

[15] On the early history of the University of Aberdeen, see John Durkan, 'Early Humanism and King's College', *Aberdeen University Review* 48 (1980), 259–79. An important primary source is Hector Boece's own *Lives of the Bishops of Mortlach and Aberdeen*, ed. James Moir (New Spalding Club, Aberdeen 1894), pp. 84–96.

[16] He was said to be dead in a supplication of 20 October 1519, Reg. Supp., 1675, ff. 111^v–112^r.

[17] *ibid.*, 1547, ff. 290^{r-v}; 1558, ff. 211^v–212^r.

[18] *ibid.*, 1604, f. 221^v.

[19] Spens was certainly rector of Conveth in November 1508, when he was elected an assessor by the Faculty of Arts at St Andrews (*Acta*, 288). But he may have given the benefice up by November 1511, when he was identified as rector of Flisk (*ibid.*, 301). According to the record of Lamb's supplication of 10 November 1519, Conveth was vacant by the resignation of 'Arthe Inzoine' (Reg. Supp., 1680, ff. 49^v–50^r).

[20] E.g. 1484, f. 282^v; 1558, ff. 211^v–212^r.

[21] *ibid.*, 1703, ff. 197^v–198^r.

[22] *ibid.*, 1734, f. 90^v; 1728, f. 256^v.

[23] *ibid.*, 2269, ff. 201^v–202^r.

[24] St Andrews University Muniments, Acta Rectorum (UY 305/1), pp. 74–7.

[25] *ibid.*, pp. 50–1.

[26] St Andrews University Muniments, St Salvator's College, Cartulary A, f. d 2^r.

[27] *Reg. Cambuskenneth*, pp. 122–3.

[28] *RMS*, iii, nos. 338, 2375; cf. *TA*, v, 245.

[29] *The Letters of James V*, ed. R. K. Hannay and Denys Hay (Edinburgh 1954), p. 191.

[30] See John Durkan and Anthony Ross OP, *Early Scottish Libraries* (Edinburgh 1961), p. 52. For the details of Lamb's ownership mark, I am indebted to Dr Durkan.

[31] Vatican Archives, Reg. Annates, 69, f. 7^v.

[32] *ibid.*

[33] Reg. Supp., 2259, ff. 192^{r-v}.

[34] *ibid.*, 2269, ff. 201^v–202^r.

[35] Vatican Archives, Brev. Lat., 23, f. 554^v.

[36] Reg. Supp., 2334, ff. 198^v–199^r; Brev. Lat., 28, 279^r–280^v.

[37] Reg. Supp., 2259, ff. 186^v–187^r. For this and the four previous references I am indebted to Mr Tom Graham.

[38] Petitioning on 23 November 1540 for a new provision to Croy and Moy, Liddell states that Lamb resigned the canonry and prebend to Pope Clement VII (who died on 25 September 1534); Reg. Supp., 2399, ff. 35^v–36^r. It is in fact clear from the protocol book of Thomas Kene, ff. 20^r–21^v, that Lamb had made this resignation by 10 January 1529; I am grateful to Dr John Durkan for this reference.

[39] *Acts of the Lords of the Council in Public Affairs*, p. 466.

[40] On the early history of the College of Justice, see RK Hannay, *The College of Justice* (Edinburgh 1933).

[41] There is a useful summary of these events in Gordon Donaldson, *Scotland: James V to James VII* (Edinburgh 1965), pp. 63–84.

[42] *Treasurer's Accts*, viii, pp. 323, 384.

[43] *Acts of the Lords of the Council in Public Affairs*, pp. 559, 574.

[44] *ibid.*, pp. 596–8. For the background to this dispute, see *ibid.*, pp. xxxii–xlv.

[45] Reg. Supp., 2704, f. 209^r, f. 210^r; 2718, f. 100^v; 2722, ff. 152^v–153^r; 2706, 205^{r-v}. Lamb is stated on 26 June 1550 to be deceased, in a document relating to the church of Conveth: *Evidence*, III, 359.

[46] *ibid.*, 2818, ff. 214^v–215^r.

[47] *ibid.*, 2849, ff. 248^{r-v}.

[48] See RG Cant, *The University of St Andrews: A Short History* (2nd edn, Edinburgh/London 1970), pp. 36–7.

[49] Haddington was evacuated between 14 and 17 September, and the stronghold at Broughty about the same time: v. WK Jordan, *Edward VI: The Young King* (London 1968), pp. 297–9.

[50] *ibid.*, pp. 506–23; ML Bush, *The Government Policy of the Protector Somerset* (London 1975), pp. 32–9. Somerset was actually deposed on 10 October, and removed from Windsor to the Tower of London four days later; allowing a little time for the news to reach Scotland, the end of October is therefore a fairly firm *terminus ad quem*, since Lamb refers to Somerset without giving any indication of his disgrace.

[51] Merriman, *op. cit.*, 24–6. Of these works three (James Henderson's *Exhortacion to the Scottes*, Somerset's own *Epistle or exhortacion to vniti & peace*, and Nicholas Bodrugan's *Epitome of the title that the Kynges Maiestie of Englande hath to the souereignitie of Scotlande*) were printed, along with the 1542 *Declaration* in JAH Murray's edition of *The Complaynt of Scotland* (EETS, London 1882), pp. 189–256.

[52] *ibid.*, pp. cviii–cxvi; the evidence is reviewed by AM Stewart in his STS edition of *The Complaynt of Scotland* (Edinburgh 1979), pp. xi–xx. Although a number of other suggestions have been made concerning the authorship, Dr Stewart argues strongly that Wedderburn was indeed the author.

[53] *Complaynt*, ed. Stewart, p. 2.

[54] *ibid.*, pp. x–xi.

[55] If the two works had been begun about the same time, in the spring or early summer of 1549, it would of course have been quite possible for Lamb to have seen all or part of the *Complaynt* in draft while working on the *Resonyng*.

[56] *STC* 9179. The text is printed by Murray, *loc. cit.*, pp. 191–206.

[57] Cf. Antonia Gransden, *Historical Writing in England: c. 1307 to the Early Sixteenth Century* (London 1982), pp. 276–7.

[58] See below, pp. 162–3.

[59] For a discussion of the textual differences between the two editions, see Denys Hay, *Polydore Vergil* (Oxford 1952), pp. 187–98.

[60] Felix Gilbert, *History: Choice and Commitment* (Cambridge, Mass./ London 1977), pp. 204–6; on the sixteenth-century reputation of Sabellico, cf. Eric Cochrane, *Historians and Historiography in the Italian Renaissance* (Chicago/London 1981), pp. 83–6 and passim; Agostino Pertusi, 'Gli inizi della storiografia umanistica nel Quattrocento', in *La Storiografia Veneziana fino al Secolo XVI: Aspetti e Problemi*, ed. Agostino Pertusi (Florence 1970), pp. 265–332, at 319–31.

[61] *Anglica Historia* (J Bebelius: Basel 1534), pp. 15–16.

[62] The legend of Gathelos, prince of Troy and Scota, the daughter of Pharaoh was used by the Scots at the beginning of the fourteenth century, and then appears in the major chroniclers from Fordoun and Bower on.

[63] *Complaynt*, ed. Stewart, pp. xxi–xxiv.

[64] For a general survey of the tradition, see Elizabeth Merrill, *The Dialogue in English Literature* (New York 1911); the vogue for dialogue in the later 1540s is discussed by John N King, *English Reformation Literature: The Tudor Origins of the Protestant Tradition* (Princeton NJ 1982), pp. 258–62, 284–92.

[65] Buonaccorso's work was also the model for a play, Henry Medwell's *Fulgens and Lucres* (*c.*1490).

[66] For Barclay's *Egloges*, see the EETS edition by Beatrice White (London 1928).

[67] See *Rede me and be not wrothe*, ed. E. Arber (London 1871).

[68] Smith, op. cit., pp. 284–92. 'A Dialogue betwixt the Gentleman and the Plowman' was among the heretical books prescribed by the English government in December 1531; *LP*, v, App. no. 18.

[69] Quintin Kennedy, *Two Eucharistic Tracts*, ed. CH Kuipers MHM (Nijmegen 1964), pp. 75–103.

[70] *The Buke of the Sevyne Sagis*, ed. CC van Buuren-Veenenbos (Leiden 1982), pp. 43–97.

[71] Lamb uses *disapoynting* only in the sense of 'the breaking of an appointment'; see Glossary.

[72] For a valuable array of examples, see these items in *DOST*.

ABBREVIATIONS

Acta	*Acta Facultatis Artium Universitatis Sancti Andree*, ed. AI Dunlop (2 vols, SHS, Edinburgh 1964)
APA 1501–54	*Acts of the Lords of Council in Public Affairs*, 1501–1554, ed. RK Hannay (Edinburgh 1932)
Cal. SP Scot.	*Calendar of State Papers Relating to Scotland*, ed. MJ Thorpe (2 vols, London 1858)
DOST	*Dictionary of the Older Scottish Tongue*
EETS	Early English Text Society
LP	*Letters and Papers of the Reign of Henry VIII*, ed. JS Brewer and J Gairdner (22 vols, London 1862–1972)
OED	*Oxford English Dictionary*
Reg. Supp.	Vatican Archives, Registra Supplicationum (microfilm held in the Department of Scottish History, University of Glasgow)
RMS	*Registrum Magni Sigilli Regum Scotorum*, ed. JM Thomson et al. (11 vols, Edinburgh 1882–1914)
SHS	Scottish History Society
SR	*Statutes of the Realm*, ed. J. Reithby et al. (12 vols, London 1810–28)
STC	*A Short-Title Catalogue of Books Printed in England, Scotland and Ireland, and of English Books Printed Abroad, 1475–1640*, ed. AW Pollard and GR Redgrave (London 1926; 2nd edn, 2 vols, London 1976–)
STS	Scottish Text Society
Treasurer's Accts	*Accounts of the Lord High Treasurer of Scotland*, ed. T Dickson et al. (11 vols, Edinburgh 1877–1916)

Ane Resonyng of ane Scottis and Inglis merchand betuix
Rowand and Lionis &c.

Compilt be Maistir William Lambe, person of Conveht and
Consull of our Souerane Ladies College of Justice,
5   bruther of M. Patric Liddale, author that this buke is cum to
knawlege of the redar.

6   cum to *MS. adds* Mennis, *deleted by scribe.*

12 'To cry cok' is a Middle Scots expression meaning to
    admit defeat; cf. Dunbar's Flyting, l. 238, 'Rottin
    crok, dirtin dok — cry cok, or I sall quell the!'
    (Poems, ed. Kinsley, p. 85), and Douglas' Aeneid, Prol.
    XI, ll. 119-20, 'Becum thow cowart, crawdoun recryand/
    And by consent cry cok, thy ded is dycht' (ed. Cold-
    well, STS, IV, 4).

f. 355^r Heir begynnis ane resonyng of Scottis and Inglis
marchand betuix Rowand and Lyonis &c.

Scottis merchand

Countra man, and it be ȝour pleisour: quhar go ȝe
to, and quhar lyis ȝour besynes?

Inglis merchand

5   I go to Lyonis. Quhat be ȝou þat speris? Be ȝow
ane Scott?

Scott.

That am I, and wald haue fallowschip be þe sam way.

Inglis.

Do ȝe nocht eschame to be callit ane Scott þir
dayis?

Scott.

10   Na, forsuyth! I do nocht knaw þat quhy ȝitt I
suld be eschamit of my natioun.

Inglis.

ȝe Scottis will neuir cry 'Cok' quhill ane of ȝow
is on lyf! Bot, guid fallow, think ȝow nocht þe
Inglismen be guid trastie men of warre and vic-
15   torius peopill, þat dois baith ruffill ȝow and þe

4   Cf. <u>The Complaynt of Scotland</u> (ed. Stewart), p. 22:

    ... the father takkis the vand or the scurge, to
    puneise his sonne, that hes brokyn his command,
    ande quhen his sonne becummis obedient, the father
    brakkis the vand ande castis it in the fyir.

Both dealing with the misdoings of the Scots at an
early stage of the argument, these two passages give
a clear indication of contact between the authors of
the two works.

11   Lamb refers to <u>A Declaration conteynyng the ivst
causes and consyderations, of this present warre with
the Scottis</u> (T. Berthelet, London 1542) /STC 9179/,
printed by Murray, pp. 191-206, and to <u>An Epistle or
exhortacion to vnitie and peace, sent from the Lord
Protector & others of the kynges moste honorable
counsall of England to the Nobilitie, Gentlemen and
Commons, and to al others the inhabitauntes of the
Realme of Scotlande</u> (R. Grafton, London 1548) /STC
9181/, printed by Murray, pp. 237-46.

13   This information is strikingly accurate: the invasion
of Scotland by English forces under the leadership of
Sir Robert Bowes took place in August 1542, but Bowes'
instructions were dated 28 July (<u>LP</u>, xvii, no. 540,
p. 312). Lamb was no doubt thinking of the worsening
crisis which led to this mobilisation.

Frenche-men?

Scott.

The Inglis dois no<u>ch</u>t ruffill ws so mekill as our
awin mishaving to God and misgyding in veirfare:
quha knawis how sone þe fathir sall thraw þe wand
5   in þe fyre quharwith he bett his childring, and how
sone þe Scottis maybe expert in weirfair?

Inglis.

ʒow do appeir juge oure weir iniust.

Scott.

ʒe, forsuyth, and no<u>ch</u>t þe Scottis alane, bot also
all vnaffecti<u>o</u>nat men, be þai Inglis, be þai
10   Frenche, or be /p̄ai̅/ Duche, as I beleif.

Inglis.

I persaue ʒow haif no<u>ch</u>t reid þe buik maid ane
thousand fyf hundre<u>th</u> fourty twa ʒeir of Christ
vpou<u>n</u> þe declaratioun of þis instant weir begun in
þe moneth of Julij of þe forsaid ʒeir be þe
15   puissant prince, King Henry þe Aucht; and also ʒow
appeir no<u>ch</u>t haif red ane vthir tractat sett fur<u>th</u>
and publist be Kyng Edwart and be þe Protecto<u>ur</u> /
f. 355^V and counsell of Ingland, þe quhilk is authorisat
and prentit at Lundoun the ane thousand fyf hun-
20   dre<u>th</u> fourty aucht ʒeiris of Christ; in þe quhilk

_____
17 þe <u>interlin. MS.</u>

twa buikis ar contenit sex iust causis of þir sevin
ʒeiris /of 7 iust weir be-tuix the Scottis and ws
Inglismen, as þe sone be iust cleir lanterne of þe
day.

Scott.

5   Quhilkis be tha just causis?

Inglis.

The first just causis is, ʒour King James the Fift
did brek his appunctit meting in ʒork with our King
Henry the Aucht. The second causs, ʒour kyng wald
no<u>ch</u>t mak rendering of ane certane Inglis rebellis,
10   fugitiuis in Scotland, at Kyng Henryis requeist.
The thrid, þe kyngis maiestate, with his greit miseiss, being cu<u>m</u>ing in mid-wintir fra Lundoun to
ʒork for to haif mett with his nephew ʒour kyng, at
þat sam tym þair wes thre or four Inglis gentill-
15   men callit Finnekis slane be þe Scottis. The ferd,
þe Scottis hes vsurpit ane pece of land on þe
marchis and boundis of Ingland. The fyift caus, þe
Scottis kyngis dois refuiss to mak obedience to
þair souerane kyng of Ingland. Thir fyif causis be
20   co<u>n</u>tenit in þe buik vpone þe declaratioun of þis
weir; the sax hes happi<u>nn</u>it laitlie sen þe begy<u>n</u>ing
of þis weir: the quhilk causis maid ws to obtene
the Greit Seill of Scotland vpone ʒour quene

---

2   of <u>MS</u>. as
23 Scotland <u>corrected in MS. from</u> Ingland

21 The English merchant addresses the unknown travellers
in French, the obvious approach on a French road.
But the horsemen either do not understand his French,
or do not speak French at all. They respond in Latin,
the medium of international communication.

heretrice mariage with our nobill kyng Edwart, the
quhilk oblising 3ow haue brokin.   Thir sam sax
causis is contenit in ane pretty buik be it-self.
Contray-man, be nocht thir or ony ane of þam just
5   causis of weir, moving quhilk all 3ow sall find
sufficientlie and autentikle provin in þe saidis
twa buikis, publist to all mennis knawlege be þe
greit and weill advysit authorite of Ingland.
Quhat sayis and jugeis 3ow of thir two buikis and
10   of þair continente?

Scott.

To juge on tha buikis, and also on the just causis
contenit in þame, I will nocht nor sall nocht tak
þe discussing þairof on me; for quhen I say ane
thing 3e will say ane vther, and swa 3e nor I
15   nothir may aggre.   Bot heireftir followis thre
horssmen: quhat-evir þai be, I am content þat ony
ane of þame be juge quhithir 3our opinioun or myne
be conforme to reasoun.

Inglis.

Be thir followaris Franche-men, than þai effectio-
20   nat be to 3ow Scottis; be thai of ony vthir natioun
than will I be content as 3ow sayis. Messieurs!
Ou aller vous, messieurs? Attendez, si vous
plaist, ung peu! Dou estoes vous?

Thre horss-men

Nescimus quid queratis.

Inglis.

Cuiates estis?

Horss-men

Sumus numdam mercatores proficiscentes Lugdunum.

Inglis.

Per comode accedit. Heir be graif wyiss neutrale
men, as apperis. Ny<u>ch</u>tbour Scott, can ȝow no<u>ch</u>t
5   speik Latin?

Scott.

Nocht mekill. Inquyre gife þir honest men speikis
and onderstandis ony vthir leid.

f. 356^r   Inglis.

Domini mei, noscis ne loqui vlla alia lingua quam
vestra vernacula et Latina lingua?

Horss-men

10   Cum adolescerimus, aliquot annos negotiati sumus
Lundoni.

Scott.

Than ȝe can speik Inglis?

―――
11 Lundoni corrected in MS. from Lugdoni

3 All three were prominent Catholic martyrs, executed
   by Henry VIII in the summer of 1535. The death of
   Sir Thomas More on 6 July was a European scandal, and
   had been preceded by those of John Fisher, bishop of
   Rochester, on 25 June, and (on 4 May) of Dr Richard
   Reynolds, a Brigittine monk of Sion, who was famous
   in his day for his piety and learning and who, along
   with three Carthusians, was among the earliest
   clerical victims of Henry's attack on his opponents
   in the Church. Lamb undoubtedly expected his readers
   to know, as the two merchants do not, that all three
   horsemen are dead.

Horss-men

We do vnderstand bettir Inglis þan we can speik.

Scott.

Guid schirris, quhat be ȝour names, and ȝe pleiss?

Thomas More

I am namit Thomas Moir, this vthir Jhon Fischear,
and this thride the father man of Sion.

Scott.

5   Guid schir of Syon, pleis ȝow heir this Inglis merchand and me comown vpone twa buikis, contenand þe
causis of þis instant weir betuix Scotland and Ingland? Howbeit ȝe haif hantit in Ingland, ȝitt ȝour
grauitie, ȝour wisdome and aige maikis me nocht
10 suspect ȝow mair affectionat to Inglismen than to
Scottis.

Guid man of Sion

Gude freindis, quhen I duelt in Ingland I hard
mekill commonyng of þe Scottis and Inglis weiris,
and als how þe sam hes continewit þir mony hun-
15 dreth ȝeiris; bot quhithir of þe twa nationis be
maist culpabill þairof, God dois knaw. Heirfor I
hald þis mater hear and weichtiar þan may be de-
cydit be me, bot swa thir twa my companionis geif

---

8 Howbeit ... Ingland added in margin

attendance to heir ȝow reasown in þe mater, I with
þair adwyiss, God willing, sall juge na wrang.

Jhone Fischear

ȝe haue done weill to entir sick commonyng, quhilk
will mak þe lang irksum way appeir schort.

Thomas Moir

5 We merchandis makis small gaine in tyme of weir!

Inglis.

Guid schiris, I say this thousand ȝeir Ingland
neuir intret so just weir as þis a contra ȝow
Scottis now, the quhilk Kyng Henry þe Aucht begouth
in þe moneth of Julij, þe ȝeir of God ane thousand
10 fyfe hundreth fourty twa ȝeiris, and þe sam oure
Protectour and Greit Counsell continewis and will
be þe grace of God mantene guidlie; for thai do
pruife þis weir just be sax reasonis and causis,
contenit in twa prettie tractatis, autenticlie
15 authorisate / and publist to all nationis. Gife
f. 356ᵛ ȝow, guid schirris, haue nocht reid þame, heir I
gife vnto ȝow, guid man of Syon, þir samyn tractatis, þat ȝe with ȝour companionis may reid þame.
Nebour Scott, I think ȝow haife red þame. I intend
20 to preif þe disapoynting of þe tway kyngis meting,
the refusall of þe kyngis rebellis randering, the

---

7   intret corrected in MS. from increst
15 authorisate repeated MS.
20 preif interlin. MS.

20 Lamb is perhaps referring to Cuthbert Tunstall,
    bishop of Durham, who was commissioned by the Council
    to prepare the English case in October 1542 (LP,
    xvii, no. 898 (ii); cf. Charles Sturge, Cuthbert
    Tunstal, Churchman, Scholar, Statesman, Admini-
    strator /London 1938/, pp. 236-7). Tunstall was
    again involved in 1548 (ibid., pp. 274-5). As in
    other points of detail, it would seem that Lamb was
    well-informed about the origins of the English
    propaganda documents.

contemptioun of þe slauchtir of þe Finnekis, the
vsurpatioun of þe Inglis ground, alanerlie be þe
deid selfe freslie done; the superiorite þat Ingland hes in Scotland I sall appruife be historyis,
5   instrumentis and recordis, with registreis. The
saxt just causis of weir salbe proponit perticular-
lie be it-selfe, and compleitlie provin. And first
of all, quhat can ȝow say, nychtbour Scott, bott
all þir tractatis ar weill sufficientlie author-
10   isate and ordourlie procedit, als by þat the causis
contenit in þame trew and just? Thir thre honest
men will abill say with þe buikis conforme to my
opinioun.

Scott.

Giffe this be maist just weir þat Ingland maid þir
15   thowsand ȝeiris a contra þe Scottis, than sall I
mak all ȝour weiris iniust, God to borrow! First
of all, I ansuer to þe authorisate autentiknes of
ȝour two tractatis: I can nocht deny bot bayth ȝour
tractatis ar autentick, becaus þe buik callit þe
20   Declaratioun of Weir wes maid be the wysast man of
Ingland, revysit be Kyng Henry þe Aucht, and þaireftir deulie prentit, as þe vthir tractat, callit
þe Exhortatioun for Vnioun of Scotland with Ingland,
is autentick becaus it is maid be þe wisdome of
25   Lundoun maturalie advysit, correctit and authorisate be þe Protectoure and be Kyng Edwardis

---

19 autentick corrected in MS. from intentick

19   'Improbatioun' is here used in the technical, legal
     sense, apparently peculiar to Scots, of disproof of
     a legal document. DOST cites this usage from 1555,
     in the records of the Justiciary Court, while OED
     has the non-technical sense of 'disproof' from 1551.
     Lamb's use of the term is thus its earliest recorded
     occurrence in either sense.

counsell. Bot, nebour, thay twa buikis of ȝouris
apperis to me nocht ordourlie procedit, becaus thai
contene þe process and finale decesioun of ane grit
wechtie, doubtabill questioun of weir fyftene hun-
5   dreth ȝeiris betuix two potent realmes.

Nebour, call ȝe ane guid ordoure of process and ane
guid sentence diffinitiue in sa wechtie, sa auld
ane mater betuix so greit parteis, þat the court of
Lundoun one þe ane part alane suld propone this
10   questioun, suld except, suld vse þair awin domistical pruife, suld concluid and als diffine þe samyn
questioun? Quhar wes þe nobilite and thre Estatis
of Ingland at þis proceding? Quhar wes Scotland,
þe vthir contrary party, the quhilk wes neuer sum-
15   mond nor requirit to se þe proponyng and proceding
and gevin of sentence vpon þis questioun? Thus be
þe absence of þe principall parteis cleirlie apperis ȝour deformit and misordourit proceding in þis
mater: my pruif of improbatioun is ȝour awin taill,
20   contenit in ȝour awin twa buikis. Now, guid man of
Syon, pleis ȝow reid thai buikis, and þaireftir ȝe
will find þe autentiknes of þir two Inglis buikis
sufficient, bot I traist þat ȝe sall bayth find and
juge ane greit misordourit proceding of þai sam twa
25   buikis, conforme to my allegeance.

Guid man of Syon

The guidnes of ane actioun may stand with ane mis-

---

6 Nebour MS. adds Scott subsequently deleted

14   Cf. <u>Declaration</u>, sig. a ii^{v} (p. 192):

     The kynge our father in that matier mynded loue,
     amitie, and perpetuall frendshyp betwene the
     posteritie of both, whiche how soone it fayled ...

18   Cf. <u>Declaration</u>, sig. a iii^{r} (p. 193):

     ... and euer we trusted, the tree wold bring
     forth good fruite, that was on thone partie of so
     good a stocke, and continually in apparance put
     forth so fayre buddes ...

ordourit proceding.

f. 357^r   Scott.

Schir, I onderstand ʒow nocht, for I haue nocht
mekill nothir of auld nor of new leirnyng, bot I
traist þair can be na thing bayth guid and evill at
5   ane tym?

Guid man of Syon

It apperis weill ʒow, Scott, be nocht leirnit þe
Lundoun way! ʒow, companʒeoun of Ingland, go fordwart to þe iust causis of þis present weir.

/Inglis./

Oure lait maistir of nobill memorie, Henry þe
10   Aucht, publist ane buik vpone þe declaratioun of
þis weir, quharof I will report heir every sub-
stantiale poynt, becaus euerilk ane hes nocht þat
buik; the quhilk sayis þat quhen Kyng Henry þe
Sevint gaif his dochtir in mariage to Kyng James þe
15   Ferd of Scotland he myndit lufe, amite and perpet-
uall freindschip betuene þe posteritie of þame
bayth. Bot how sone did it begin to faill!

Scott.

I say it begouth to faill at þe rute, Kyng Henry þe
Sevint. For quhen twa or thre ʒeiris eftir þat

---

9   Heading om. MS.
16   posteritie corrected in MS. from prosperite

1   Sir Robert Kerr of Ferniehurst was murdered by English
     borderers, an outrage which affected Anglo-Scottish
     relations for some time. Most details of the incident
     are obscure; older writers give the date as 1511, but
     that is clearly impossible since Wolsey wrote to Henry
     VIII on the subject in April 1508 (Letters of James IV,
     no. 171), and the correct date would appear to have
     been shortly before 6 November 1500 (LP, i, p. 960).
     Lamb's information implicating a man named Starhead is
     not wholly inaccurate, but the instigator of the crime
     was probably the Bastard Heron, assisted by two ser-
     vants named Starhead and Lilburn. See Calendar of
     Border Papers, ii, 565 (an account dated 1598); Howard
     Pease, The Lord Wardens of the Marches of England and
     Scotland (London 1913), pp. 31-2; and W. Scott, Bor-
     der Antiquities of England and Scotland (2 vols, London
     1889), pp. xlviii-xlix, cxvii. Scott states, without
     giving an authority, that Starhead was killed at York,
     not Durham. The case was the subject of a letter from
     James IV to Henry VIII, dated 26 July 1513 (Letters of
     James IV, no. 560).

20   The head of St John the Baptist was a celebrated relic,
     kept in the church of St-Silvestre at Amiens, where it
     had been brought from Constantinople in 1206. James
     Hamilton, created earl of Arran in 1503, was being held
     in England by April 1508 (Letters of James IV, no. 171)
     and was still there on 10 May 1509, when he attended
     the funeral of Henry VII (LP, i, no. 20). He witnessed
     the Anglo-Scottish treaty of 29 August 1509 (ibid., no.
     153), and was back in Edinburgh by 29 November (ibid.,
     no. 255), having perhaps returned with the Scottish
     ambassadors.

mariage happy<u>nn</u>it ane nobill Scottis kny<u>ch</u>t, Schir
Robert Ker, be slane nocht honestlie be ane Inglis-
man callit Starret, and þaireftir detenit and mantenit in Ingland, and Kyng Henry þe Sevint, being
5   requirit be his sone, kyng of Scotland, for justice, ansuerit how Sterrett, þe comittar of þat
slauchtir, wes fugitiue furth of all Ingland, howbeit in verite þe samy<u>n</u> man drew his hald and
duelling about Durhame fra þe bordouris of Ingland,
10 quhar ane Scottis-man outlaw callit ⌐   ⌐
fand and brocht þe samyn Sterrettis heid fra
Durhame to Kynge James þe Ferd and obtenit þairfore his pardoun of certane crymes. This Carris
slauchtir is provin be þe bordouraris of Ingland
15 and Scotland; the refusell of justice is provin be
fyve sundre wryttingis of Kyng Henry þe vij.
direct<u>it</u> to his sone, Kyng James þe Ferd (ȝit þir
wryttingis ar remanand in our Register); also ane
thousand in Ingland and als mony in Scotland re-
membris þe maner of Sterrettis heid-cutting and
20 also co<u>n</u>voying fra Durhame. Secundlie, James, erle
of Arrane, returnyng in Scotland be se fra his
pilgramage of Sanct Jhone in Amianis, beand drevin
be tempest in Ingland, was thair foure ȝeiris
detint, and wes no<u>ch</u>t fred for na requeist of þe
25 guid-sone, nor for sindre ambaxatouris sending, nor
for reasoun of leag and amite þan laitlie maid at
þe mariage of þis Inglis dochtir, quhilk proportis

---

7   furth <u>repeated MS.</u>
10 <u>lacuna in MS.</u>

13   There is no mention of a bequest to Queen Margaret in
     the printed version of Henry VII's will (LP, i, no. 1)
     but there can be no doubt that the issue was a real
     one, particularly in 1512-13. James IV and Margaret
     both wrote to Henry VIII on the subject in April 1513
     (Letters of James IV, nos. 543, 546).

19   The point of this remark is obscure, as is the iden-
     tity of the gentlemen cited by Lamb. But he is right
     on one point: neither Denny nor Herbert was among the
     executors of Henry VII's will.

þat ane stormested schip or man suld haue fre
passage throw athir Ingland or Scotland. This lang
detining of þe erle of Arrane, cousing germane of
James þe Ferd, and þis present Gouernouris father,
5   and als refusall of his libertie, may be provin be
sindre nobillis and courticianis ȝitt on lyfe,
bayth of Ingland and Scotlandis court, and also
provin be tuenty excusatorijs writtingis of Kyng
Henry þe Sevint directit to his guid-sone, Kyng
10   James þe Ferd.

I haue said to ȝow, nichtbour, quhat sap come fra
the rute: now sall ȝe heir þe fruit of þe self tre
f. 357ᵛ and branche. Mergaret, quene of / Scotland, being
to hir left be Kyng Henry þe Sevint, hir father,
15   ane honest legacy for ane taikin of bettir memorie,
scho nor hir husband culd nevir attene þe samyn
fra Kyng Henry the Aucht, thair brothir. Nebour,
ȝe will abill ansuer þat þe stop heirof wes becaus
Henry the vij. maid nocht Schir Antony Denny and
20   Schir William Harbret jugis of his testament,
quhilkis we call executouris; or peraduentour ȝe
will nocht blame Kyng Henry þe Aucht for this leg-
acyis detentioun, for gife he had delyuerit þat
legacie to þe Scottis quene, than þair suld nocht
25   haif bene sufficient mony for to recompance and to
restore þe iniust vnlawis, exactionis tane vnder
þe pretence of justice fra þe baronis and comunis
of Ingland, quharof Kyng Henry þe Aucht maid con-

_____
20 Harbret corrected in MS. from Henry

4   The siege of Tournai, in the county of Hainault, took
    place between 15-23 September 1513, resulting in a
    victory for the English.

11 Thomas, lord Dacre and Nicholas West, dean of Wind-
    sor were appointed ambassadors on 15 April 1512 (LP
    i, no. 1169 (xiv)); there is no record of an offer
    to make James Henry's heir.

18 Henry Courtenay, the grandson of Edward IV through
    his daughter Catherine, was not created marquis of
    Exeter until 1525. It was apparently claimed by
    some of Exeter's supporters (in 1531) that he would
    succeed to the throne: this was revived against him
    when he was arrested and attainted in 1538 (LP, xiii,
    no. 961). He was beheaded on 9 January 1539.

26 Surrey was preparing an army against Scotland by 1
    August 1512 (LP, i, no. 1317), but there is no
    record of large-scale fighting at that time. On 20
    October 1513, Dacre referred to a raid in Teviotdale
    'in the last war', but it is not clear that this
    applies to the previous year's campaign (ibid., i,
    no. 2382).

science _and_ commandit in his testament sic exactionis to be restorit to the awnaris; or abill
ȝe will say þat mony men of Ingland thocht þat mony
wes bettir bestowit one þe wyn̲ing of Torna in

5   Haino. This legacie is provin be Kyng Henry the
vij. testament; the refusale þairof is provin be
ambaxatouris and sindre writtingis of Kyng Henry
the Aucht to his brothir and sistir of Scotland.

Forther, Kyng Henry the Auch, preparand his first

10 army _a contra_ France, for to haue his guid-brothir
mair hartlie, send ambaxatouris declarand his
passage in France and how God had no̲c̲h̲t provydit
ane air of his body, tharfor him-self had concludit to caus his sistir-sone of Scotland, quha

15 wes nerrast of lyn to him, be declarit apperand
air of Ingland in Parliament. Bot, nebour, in
plane _a contra_ a-foir his passage than in France
he causit þe marquess of Excestre be declarit air
in Ingland. The first part heirof may be provin

20 be þe ambaxatou̲r̲is ȝit on lyfe, _and_ also be sindre
writingis of Kyng Henry þe Aucht, direct bayt̲h̲ to
his sistir and guid-brothir, remanand in þe Scottis
Register; for witnessing and preif þat þe marques
of Excestre wes declarit þan apperand air, þe act

25 of ȝour Parliement proportis. Nebour, also remember þe raid of Ettale or þe first passing of
Kyng Henry þe viij. in Fra̲n̲ce, at þe quhilk tym þe
Inglismen draif þe guidis of Merss and Teviothdaill
aboue the valour of xx^m lib., and eftir sindre

30 requisitionis na redress maid tharfor; a fyve

11 Cf. <u>Declaration</u>, sig. a ii^{r} (p. 191):

    The Kyng of Scottes our Nephieu and neighbour,
    whom we in his youth and tender age preserued
    and maynteyned from the great dangier of other,
    and by our authoritie and power conduced hym
    sauely to the riall possession of his estate ...

22 The meeting of 'the Field of the Cloth of Gold' took
    place between Henry VIII and Francis I near Ardres,
    7-20 June 1520. For a full account of the occasion,
    see Joycelyne G. Russell, <u>The Field of Cloth of Gold:</u>
    <u>Men and manners in 1520</u> (London 1969).

hundreth on Ingless bordour and als mony Scottis
previs þis raid and refusale of redress. Nebour,
thir be þe fruit of þe tre cuming of sa guid ane
nobill stok; heir be the lufe, amite and mony
5   strenge behavoris from þe guid-brothir of Ingland
to þe guid-brothir of Scotland. Nebour, wald þis
vnkyndlie fruit haue þe stomok movit maid of a
stane, nocht onlie þe he curage of ane ʒung prince
as Kyng James þe Fyft!

Inglis.

10   Countra man, ʒow seikis ferdar than is requirit to
oure purpoiss. Did nocht Kyng Henry þe Aucht pre-
f. ₃58^{r} serue, mantene from grit / danger, the tendir age
of ʒour kyng, James þe Fyft, and conducit him sauflie to þe riale possessioun of Scotland?

Scott.

15   Quhat ʒow call mantening and conducing I knaw nocht,
bot ane thing is weill knawin: þat nothir Inglisman
nor woman fra his birth to his deith reparit about
him, and quhar sic naturale deutie of personage wes
nocht vsit, as ʒe haue hard, quha can beleif þat
20   King Henry þe viij. vsit liberalite towart his
nepot?

Call ʒe preserving ʒour kyng for to pas to Ardress

---

6   to ... Scotland added in margin
9   Fyft corrected in MS. from Ferd
12   grit repeated MS.

1   Henry VIII met Francis I at Boulogne on 21 October
    1532 (<u>LP</u>, v, nos 1484-5); cf. <u>The maner of the</u>
    <u>tryumphe at Caleys and Bulleyn</u> (W. de Worde: London
    1532).

4   Lamb's chronology is here becoming a little confused,
    perhaps as a result of the interpolation of the 1532
    meeting into the sequence of events. The invasion of
    the Duke of Norfolk (then still Earl of Surrey) took
    place in September 1523 after a summer of border
    raids. For an account of these events, see R.G.
    Eaves, <u>Henry VIII's Scottish Diplomacy, 1513-1524</u>
    (New York 1971), pp. 129-41.

9   Albany had sailed from Dumbarton on 27 October 1522
    (<u>LP</u>, iii, no. 2645), and Henry attempted to exploit
    his absence by concluding a peace. He was supported
    by his sister, the dowager Queen Margaret, but the
    Scottish magnates proved resistant, believing that
    Albany would return with French reinforcements. He
    did not actually arrive back in Scotland, however,
    until 21 September, two days before the burning of
    Jedburgh.

25 Lamb must be thinking of Archibald Douglas, earl of
    Angus, who with his brother, Sir George, and others
    was exiled in December 1528, and who did not return to
    Scotland until January 1543, shortly after the death
    of James V.

j^m v^c xx. and syne to Ballonӡe j^m v^c xxxiij ӡeir
of Christ, and þair appunctit ane amite and leag
with Kyng Francise of France and causit him deturne
fra þe auld leag and amite of Scotland; and þair-
5   eftir incontinent send Thomas, duik of Norfok with
xv^m weirmen in Teviothdaill, þair to birne þe toun
and abbay of Jedburgh, cast doun nyn or ten castellis and haldis of his sistir-sonis, beand of sax
or sevin ӡeiris of aige, the Scottis Gouernour,
10   Jhone, duik of Albanie, beand haldin in France be
þe said appoyntmentis, als stryif and discord
reageing amangis þe nobillis of Scotland? That at
þe two metingis of þe tuo kyngis wes appunctit the
forsaid leag and detenyng of our Gouernour þe tym
15   þat þe duik of Norphok wastit Teviothdaill is
notour, and nedis na vthir pruif þan þe deid selff.

The birning of Jedburgh abbay and castellis at þat
samyn tym is provit be þe brint wallis; and be þe
appoyntit deteyning of Jhone, duik of Albany in
20   France apperit þat ӡour kyng socht, as all ӡour
vthir kyngis before labourit, that na wyiss nor
expert man of weir suld ringne or gyd þe Scottis-
men, for na man at þat tym wes mair expert in weirfair þan þe said duik of Albany.

25   Nebour, call ӡe conducing to riale possessioun for
to mantene and defend continewalie xv. ӡeiris nobillis fugitivis of Scotland lying alwayis in a

---

1   syne corrected in MS. from fyue

4   James V was born on 10 April 1512, and was therefore
     only eleven at the time of the burning of Jedburgh.
     But Lamb may be thinking also of the border raids
     which took place over the winter of 1532-33, after
     the meeting at Boulogne; the account is less clear
     than his general command of the facts would lead us
     to expect.

22   Cf. Declaration, sig. a ii^V (p. 192):

          It hath ben very rarely and seldom seen before,
          that a king of Scottis hath had in mariage a
          doughter of Englande ...

vait, quhen þe vncle micht noy þe nephew; and als
ȝour kyng for to returne agane in France and þair
appoynt þat Kyng Francis sall nocht ayd Kyng James
þe Fyift of Scotland, and incontinent þaireftir þe
5 vncle to weir neir a ȝeir vpone þe nepot of xv. or
xvj. ȝeir of aige, haifand þan laitlie entres to þe
governyng of his realme?

The mantenyng of þe Scottis nobillis fugitiveis,
the secund meting with Francise, and also þe weir
10 sustenit, defendit be þe four quartaris of Scotland
every tym þair quartar about, is bettir knawin nor
nedis ony pruif. This is þe vncles conducing of þe
nepot to possessioun of reale estait; bot þe vncle
at þat tym seing na guid success of his weir ap-
15 punctit a pece, leage and amite for the langar
leuear of himself and his nepote. This pece is
provin be þe Greitt Seill of Ingland in our Registre; bot how lang indurit it, and quha vthir brak
it bot þe vncle?

f. 358ᵛ   Inglis.

20 Oure souerane kyng, Henry the viij., traistit and
belevit þat the tre come on þe ane part off ane
guid stok suld haue brocht furth bettir fruit, for
saldin wes it sene befoir þat ane Scottis kyng had
in mariage a dochtir of Ingland.

                    Scott.

25 Pairt of fruit of þat ȝour nobill stok, and also of

14 Cf. <u>Declaration</u>, sig. a iii^r (p. 193):

> And therfore hauynge a message sente vnto vs
> the yere paste from our sayde Nephieu, and a
> promyse made for the repayring of the sayd kyng
> of Scottis vnto vs to Yorke, and after great
> preparation on our parte made therfore, the
> same metyng was not onely disappoynted ...

Henry was seeking a meeting with James as early as
October 1534, when Lord William Howard was appointed
as ambassador to Scotland with instructions to make
the necessary arrangements (<u>LP</u>, vii, no. 1350). The
Earl of Angus wrote on 24 March 1536 indicating that
such a meeting was intended (ibid., x, no. 536), but
on 14 April James denied in an interview with Howard
that he had agreed to go to York (ibid., no. 729).
A meeting was eventually arranged for 23 September
(ibid., xi, no. 809), but it never took place. The
outrage of the English is apparent in a document of
December 1541 (<u>Cal. S.P. Scot.</u>, i, 41). Cf. also,
<u>Letters of James V</u>, pp. 316-8.

þe riale branchis, I haue rehersit; bot seir sindlare wes it sene þat the heretrice of Scotland
marijt sick ane kyng of Ingland, commit of sic stok
as he is. God will no<u>ch</u>t suffir sic bastard seid
5   to ringne, and quhat his father wes I traist þe
wallis of every guid toun will tell quhar abbayis
stuid. I will no<u>ch</u>t 3o<u>ur</u> lordis and ladyis˙re-
herss, quhilkis for þe trew<u>th</u> wes miserablie mur-
dreit, þair airis disherist, the spuil3e of 3o<u>ur</u>
10   kirkis, the extorsioun of þe 3emanrie and gentill-
men; as concerny<u>ng</u> the faith and religioun, thair
actis and proclamatiounis 3eirlie ane aganis ane
vthir will speik quhone we be gane.

                    Inglis.

3our kyng send ane familiar message and desyrit
15   oure kyng, his vncle, to appunct a meting at 3ork,
the quhilk our kyng did keip with greit inco<u>mm</u>odite
of his persoun in myd-wintir. Quhy suld 3o<u>ur</u> kyng
disapoynt the sam in greit co<u>n</u>tempny<u>ng</u> of our
kyngis maiestie?

                    Scott.

20   Nebour, 3e appeir nocht to knaw þe mater. Oure
kyng neuer send nor desyrit sic meting, bot þe contrar is plane: sick meting wes desirit, solistit
and menit quietlie be 3o<u>ur</u> kyng in sick sort that
no<u>ch</u>t aboue thre Scottis-men of þe Prevay Chalmer

-----

20 þe <u>MS. reads</u> Lundoun (<u>deleted by scribe</u>)

5 This campaign actually took place in July-September
   1536, but otherwise Lamb's account is fairly
   accurate. For reliable modern discussion of these
   events, see Karl Brandi, The Emperor Charles V,
   trans. C.V. Wedgwood (London 1939), pp. 375-81; Rene
   Guerdan, Francois I: Le Roi de la Renaissance (Paris
   1976), pp. 326-34.

19 But in fact Henry declared England neutral in August
    1536 (LP, xi, no. 330), which was reported to the
    Emperor by Chapuys on 25 August (ibid., no. 358). It
    is not clear what basis Lamb had for his suggestion
    that it was with a view to exploiting French dis-
    comfiture by reviving the English claim to the crown
    of France that Henry sought a meeting with James V.

knew þat appoynting. Nebour, I will schew schortlie quhy 3our kyng did aggrege þe breiking of þat
meting. Therfore I sall declare the just causis
of þe disapoynting: the j^m v^c xxxv.· 3eir of Christ,

5   Charlis Imperatour conducit xxxv^m guidlie men of
weir fra Geneua in Italie be se in Provincia, haif-
and one his left hand Rodanus, þe greit fluid, vnpassabill bot be grit weschell, haifing in his face
Kyng Francise with þe greit stranglie power of

10 France starklie parkit, haifand on his richt hand
þe hiddouis montanis of Savoy, his furnissing impeschit be tempest of sey; and seand his partie
refuiss battale, he postponit that his purpoiss to
a bettir tym and mair commodius place, quhilk pur-

15 poiss apperit wes to assel3e Pareiss, þe heid toun
and hert of France, or ellis for constrane þe
Frenche-men to gife battell, the quhilk purpoiss
almaist followit in deid eftir. Of þe quhilk purpoiss 3our kyng, Henry þe viij., suddanlie consauit

20 ane commodius tym, as send be þe providence of God,
for to callange his richt and titill of France;
for all Inglis kyngis awaitis alwayis a commodius

f. 359^r tym and concurrence for to / recouer þair pretendit
richt to þe croun of France. Heirfore nochtwith-

25 standing þe greit amite, þe twa forsaid hertlie
metingis, þe leag and confideratioun maid for his
awin and Kyng Francise lyiftyme, 3it he concludit
for to tak þe concurrence of Charlis þe Impera-

---

23 to repeated MS.
24 France interlin. MS.

16 The excommunication of Henry VIII was approved by
the Papal consistory in January 1536.

touris weir aganis France, and þat þe mair puissantlie and suirlie he mycht vse þis concurrence,
ʒour kyng desirit, solistit and menit prevalie ane
meting with his nephew, kyng of Scotland, as apper-
5   it to brek him fra France and for to mantene the
novationis þan maid laitlie in Ingland of heresye.
The cuming of Charlis Imperatour with his army in
Province is notourlie knawin; the maner of Kyng
Henry þe viij. proceding at þis tyme and his deidis
10   eftir following makis presumptioun quhar his mynd
was þan to France and to his nephew of Scotland.

Heir now, nebour, the causis quhy the said meting
wes disapunctit: it semit nocht to ane kyng to
interpryss a departing furth of his realme without
15   þe adwyiss of his Thre Estatis; it semit nocht a
Catholik kyng to intercommown with a kyng seuerit
fra societie of Christiṅ men; also, suld a kyng
treat and concluid greit materis without his
Estatis, quhilkis behuvit bene done gife þe meting
20   at ʒork had haldin? Suld a kyng of Scotland, haif-
and na air, beand apperand air to Ingland, entir in
familiaritie with a hosill court quhayis dedis
schamit þame nocht nouthir guidlie nor honest be
quhat way þai procure realmis to þair nepotis and
25   freindis? Heir nedis nocht to be rehersit þe last
Kyng Richard of Ingland and his brotheris departing
from þis wardill, nor nedis be rehersit þe actis of
ʒour Parliament geving and transfferring þe richt

5/6 and for ... novationis repeated and deleted MS.

7   Catherine of Aragon died on 8 January 1536. Rumours
    that she had been murdered were evidently current at
    the time: Charles V reported the fact to the Empress
    on 1 February (LP, x, no. 230). The Duke of Richmond
    died in June, having apparently been regarded as a
    possible successor to the throne, despite his il-
    legitimacy. On one point Lamb exaggerates: Henry
    married Jane Seymour on 30 May, eleven days after the
    execution of Anne Boleyn.

12 For the shape-shifting of Proteus, a popular figure
    from Classical mythology, see Virgil, Georgics, iv,
    405-14; Ovid, Fasti, i, 367-70.

of þe croun of Ingland fra ane to ane vthir, maid
in Kyng Henry þe viij. tyme, fra Lady Marie to
Elizabeth, Anna Bolonis dochtir, fra Elizabeth to
Edward, sone to Jan Symmer, Annas _pellex_ and dela-
5   trice, no<u>ch</u>t without greit periure of all þe haill
realme, now suering with Anna to be trew to hir
seid bastard borne (Quene Katherine beand on lyif
till sche wes poysonit, and þe duik of Rochemound
quhome the kyng tho<u>ch</u>t suld ringne), and on þe
10   morne eftir Annas heding succedit ane sponsit quene
of Ingland. Swa ʒe do transforme ʒour estait ryale
als oft as Protheus did change formis. Ferther,
þair wes neu<u>er</u> desyrit ane meting be-for þis tym be
þe vncle.

15   Nychtbour, now may ʒe se þat þis meting at ʒork wes
no<u>oh</u>t desyrit for luif, bot þat þe samyn wes mair
disapunctit þan þe inductioun of the twa or thre
meinʒeonis did prevalie appunct; and also ʒe may se
becaus þe nephew wald no<u>ch</u>t mak ane meting for to
20   entir new leag preiudiciale baith to his awin realme
and France, nor wald mak seductioun fra þe obseruance of þe Apostolic Sait nor wald mantene þe new
fassoun of Ingland, the vncle disburdonit his inwart displesour and greif be entering of ane inex-
25   tinguabill weir vpon his nephew and his realme,
f. 359^v quharthrow þe puissance of his / nephewis realme
micht be debilitate and waikit, to þe effect þe

---

11   do   <u>MS. has</u> conforme ʒour estait ryale als,
     <u>deleted by scribe.</u>

4   Cf. <u>Declaration</u>, sig. a iii^r (p. 193):

    ... the same metyng was not onely disappoynted,
    but also at our being at Yorke, in the lieu
    therof, an inuasion made by our said Nephieu
    his subiectis into our realme, declaringe an
    euident contempt and dispite of vs ...

7   Roger and George Fenwick were English keepers of
    Tynedale and Redesdale. Roger was murdered on 3
    March 1537 by 'three naughty persons' who fled into
    Scotland (<u>LP</u>, xii, 1, nos 596, 777). It is clear
    from the contemporary documents that the assassins
    were in fact English: Lamb seems to have added the
    charge that Scots were responsible, since it does not
    appear in the <u>Declaration</u>.

11 James may or may not have been hunting at the time,
    although it is scarcely germane to the accusation.

22 Cf. <u>Declaration</u>, sig. a iii^v (p. 193):

    And albeit the kyng of Scottis hauynge contrary
    to tharticle of the leage of amitie, receyued and
    entreteigned suche rebelles, as were of the chief

innouationis of Ingland suld no<u>ch</u>t be interrupit
nor his purpoiss <u>a contra</u> France empeschit be his
nephew.

Inglis.

3our kyng no<u>ch</u>t onlie disapoyntit þe meting, bot
5   also, oure kyng being cum̲it to 3ork for þe obser-
uing of þe same meting, in þat mene-tyme 3our kyng
and his subiectis maid inuasioun in Ingland and
slew certane Fynix, Inglis gentill-men.

Scottis.

At this slauchtir tym specifeit be 3ow, the Scottis
10   kyng come no<u>ch</u>t neir þe Inglis bordouris be lx. or
lxxx. score of mylis, for he wes þan in þe inwart
partis of Scotland at his progress of hunting; als
he ne<u>ue</u>r knew þe inuasioun and slauchtir of 3o<u>ur</u>
Fenix quhill it wes procurit be Inglis-mennis
15   selffis and executit be Scottis leud men. For our
kyngis hunting at þat tyme thare is na vthir prufe
than all Scotland; this slauchtir in þe said mater
is pruvit be ane vikit wse obseruit betuix þe bor-
do<u>ur</u>is bayt<u>h</u> of Ingland and Scotland, quhen for
20   dredour of justice thai causs quietlie outlandismen for to rub or slay þair awin ny<u>ch</u>tbouris.

Inglis.

3our kyng <u>a contra</u> þe leag maid betuix him and his
vncle resauit and intertenit certane Inglis rebel-

and principle, in sterringe the insurrection in
the North agaynst vs, with refusal before tyme,
vpon request made to restore the same ...

8   The Scottish ambassador Thomas Bellenden noted in
    July 1541 that there was concern in England about
    'certane gray freres, uther doctouris and religious
    men, quhilkis he allegis his soverane lordis rebellis
    and ressett wythin the reaulme of Scotland' (LP, xvi,
    no. 1034). Henry VIII had in fact written to James V
    on the matter at the beginning of February 1540,
    giving a list of English fugitives in Scotland which
    included Tunstall's former chaplain Dr Richard
    Hilliard, now staying in the household of Cardinal
    Betoun (LP, xv, no. 136; cf. Hamilton Papers, no. 54).
    Others on the list who may have been clerics are
    Nicholas Musgrave (said to be at Deer) and John
    Priestman (at Newbattle); a very similar list (Ham-
    ilton Papers, no. 106) also includes 'onne Arkryges',
    chantor of Cartmell, now at Holyrood.

19 Cf. Declaration, sig. a iii^v-iv^r (pp. 193-4)

    ... being for our part chalenged a piece of our
    grounde, playnly vsurped by the Scottes, and of
    no great value, being also for the same shewed
    such euidence, as more substanctiall, more
    autentique, more playne and euydent, can not be
    broughte fourthe for any parte of grounde within
    our realme ... And yet it was soo auncient, as
    it coulde not be counterfaite nowe, and the
    value of the grounde so lytell, and of so smal
    wayte, as no man wolde haue attempted to falsifie

lis, with þe refusale to rander þame at þe requeist
of his vncle, oure kyng.

Scott.

Countray-man, ʒe speik no<u>ch</u>t warlie in the randering of þir ʒour Inglis outlay-maen, for ʒe not ʒo<u>u</u>r
5   prince of greit seueritie, quhilk ʒe mene wes no<u>ch</u>t
saciate in vij. or viij. ʒeris persecutioun and
scheddin of his awin subdittis bluid.   Trewt<u>h</u> is,
in þe tyme of þat persecutioun v. or sax auld men-
dicant freris, prestis, prechouris and techeraris
10   of spirituale jurisdictioun, seikand saffete of
þair lyif, enterit in þe Scottis sanctuarye, inuiolate amangis ws vnto this day, and þai remanit
thre or four ʒeiris; and albeit thai had co<u>mm</u>ittit
trasoun <u>a contra</u> Scotland we culd no<u>ch</u>t be law haif
15   drawin þame furth of þe sanctuarie.   Be þe lik ansuer ʒour kyng, thre or four ʒeiris befor þis instant weir, wes satisfeit; the deid self previs
þis.

Inglis.

Quhat say ʒe to þe vsurping of oure landis and mer-
20   chis of Ingland, challangit be oure co<u>mm</u>issionaris
vpone þe ground, provin be ane plane evident, and
restorance þairof refusit be ʒour kyng?   We grantit
bot thre or four aikiris of barrate mure of sobir

---

6   saciate <u>corrected in MS. from</u> sociate

for suche a matier.

This passage refers to the dispute over the lands of
Cannaby (Canonbie), which had arisen as early as
October 1531 (<u>APA 1501-54</u>, pp. 362, 370, 373) and which
gave rise to hostilities in the West Marches in 1533
(<u>LP</u>, vi, no. 310). Negotiations continued during the
summer and ended with the agreement of a truce on 1
October 1533 (ibid., no. 1196).

13   'He who wants to abandon friendship seeks reasons.'
      I have not been able to locate this proverb, which
      has the ring of a lawyers' tag.

17   Cf. <u>Declaration</u>, sig. a iv^r (p. 194):

      And yet this deniall being in this wyse made vnto
      our Commissioners, they neuer the lesse by our
      commandement departed as frendes, from the
      Commissioners of Scotlande, takyng order as hath
      ben accustomed for good rule vpon the borders in
      the meane tyme ... the lorde Maxwell, warden of
      the west marches of Scotland, made proclamation
      for good rule, but yet added therwith, that the

f. 360^r valoure; bot þe ⌐more⌐ it be of sobir qua̲ntite and
          valour, þe refusale þairof is þe more inexcusabill.

                           Scott.

          To this fourt causs of weir I speir: quhen diuerss
          opinionis occurris betuix twa parteis vpone þe
     5   validitie and inualiditie of ane evide̲nt, quha suld
          juge þairupone? Sen þat mater culd no̲c̲h̲t be dis-
          cussit be commissionaris of baith þe realmes, suld
          ȝo̲u̲r kyng haue bene partie and also juge in his
          awin causs? And, geifand at þat same pece land had
     10   pertenit to Ingland, suld ȝour kyng haue mouit so
          haistie crewell weir for ane thing of so sobir
          valour, quhilk als wes no̲c̲h̲t challangit ij^c ȝeir̲i̲s̲
          befor þat tyme? Causas querit qui ab amicitia
          discedere vult. The pruif heirof is þe sobir
     15   valour of þe ground, and ij^c ȝeiris vnchanlangit
          befor.

                          Inglis.

          Eftir the refusale to restore þe thre or four
          aikiris of mure, commissionaris of baith þe realmes
          did proclame þat guid ordour suld be keipit and
     20   obseruit, as wes accustu̲m̲mat for guid reule on þe
          bordouris, and siclik Lord Maxwell, Warden of þe
          Scottis West Merch̲i̲s̲, did proclame guid ordo̲u̲r;
          bot he addit in his proclamatioun that the bor-

          ───────────────
           1   valoure sobir repeated MS.
               more MS. mure
          22 Merchis added in margin MS.

bourderers of Scotlande shuld withdrawe their
goodes from the bourders of Englande: And in-
continentely after the Scottishe men bourdurers,
the fourth of July, entred into our realme
sodeynly, and spoyled our subiectes, contrary
to our leages, euen after suche extremitie, as
it had bene in tyme of open warre. Whereat we
moche maruailed, and were compelled therfore to
furnishe our bourdour with a garrison for defence
of the same.

douraris of Scotland suld ·withdraw þair guidis
from the bordouris of Ingland, and incontinent
þaireftir þe Scottis bordouraris enterit in Ingland, spuilȝeit our subiectis a contra þe leagis
5   maid betuix the kyngis, quharat Kyng Henry merualit mekill and wes compellit þairfore to furneiss þe Inglis bordouraris with a garnesoun of
defence.

Scott.

Nebour, þocht ȝour buik culd pruif þis our War-
10   danis proclamatioun, ȝit þe sam is ane insuffi-
cient caus of presumptioun of weir, and als so
waiklie handillit þat þe verite burstis out of
euerye taill to þame þat knawis þe customis of
bayth the realmes. The Lord Maxwell did proclame
15   guid reule and addit þat the Scottis suld withdraw
þair guidis from þe bordouris of Ingland: it is
notourlie knawin þat na lord, prince nor wardan in
Scotland durst at þat tyme mak sic a restrikit
proclamatioun, for sic obedience had Kyng James þe
20   Fyift, quha at þat tyme had na occasioun to mynd
weir.

Also nychtbour, mak ȝour buik of Declaratioun
specifie the Scottis bordouraris namis, and at
quhat bordour of Ingland thai enterit, and quhat
25   guidis and quhat Inglis-men þai spuilȝeit: thair-
eftir þir allegit Scottis raidis and spuilȝeis of
Ingland will appeir mair just causis of weir and

15 Cf. Declaration, sig. a iv^V (p. 194):

    ... and in a rode made by syr Robert Bowes for
    a reuenge therof, the same sir Robert Bowes with
    many other taken prysoners ...

19 The capture of Bowes, among almost five hundred
    English prisoners, was reported on 24 August 1542
    (LP, xvii, nos 662-3). The Earl of Angus estimated
    the total strength of the English force at 3000
    (ibid., no. 673).

26 Learmonth was in London by 1 August 1542; his poor
    treatment there was reported by the French ambassa-
    dor, Charles de Marillac (LP, xvii, no. 571), but
    according to Chapuys (ibid., no. 586) this was the
    consequence of the killing on English soil of 42
    Englishmen. For a statement of the Scottish case,
    see BL MS. Royal 18 B vi, fol. 141^V (ibid., nos 643-
    4); the English version is given in the Declaration,

f. 360^v will mak me haif mater for to impruif þe / sam gife
I may.

Also ʒe sall vnderstand þat the ryding and spuil-
ʒeis of prevate Scottis and Inglis vsis to be re-
5 drest at wardan courtis, and sic radis and spuil-
ʒeis is na sufficient causs for to mak weir. Bot
gife ʒe say þat þe redress of sic guidis wes askit,
and refusit be þe Scottis Wardan, I grant þat the
ryding and spulʒeis committit be athir of þe
10 realmes wardanis or lieutennent onlie brekis þe
trewis and pece eftir þe obseruit law of bayth
Ingland and Scotland, and gife our kyngis wardanis
or lieutennentis maid þir allegit spulʒeis, than
ʒour kyng did iustlie furneiss his borderaris with
15 garnesoun. Bot ʒour kyng without ony of þir forsaid caussis send Schir Robert Bowis as his lieutennent with ane guidlie garnesoun to mak raiddis
and waisting in Scotland as a preparatiue befor
weir. This is provin be Schir Robert Bowis talkin
20 at Haldan Rig in Scotland with ane cumpany of v^m
Inglis-men of August þe xxij., the ʒeir of God j^m
v^c xlij., as begyning of iniust weir declarit be þe
justnes of God, quha will send ane semblable end of
sic ane entirit weir quhon He thinkis tym. Bot for
25 all þis, our kyng wald nocht reput þe pece-breiking
bot send Schir James Leirmonth to inquire giue his
vncle wald nocht keip þe appoyntit leag and amitie
for þe langar leuear of þame twa.   This Schir

---

1 þe repeated MS.

sig. a iv^{r-v} (p. 194).

5   'Guid Scalco' is Erik Godschalk (Godescalcus), who
    was sent by Charles V to Ireland and Scotland, to
    encourage rebellion in the former and to persuade
    James V to marry Princess Mary of England. The
    Emperor's letter to James requesting credence for
    his ambassador was sent on 24 April 1534 (MS. Royal
    18 B vi, fol. 212^r; LP, vii, no. 437), and Godschalk
    was in Scotland from October to December (Cal. S.P.
    Scot., v, 296, 374).

8   The four-month-old Princess Elizabeth was declared
    Henry VIII's heir in the session of Parliament which
    began on 15 January 1534: v. SR, iii, 471-4. The
    statute was available to Lamb in the printed version,
    published by Thomas Berthelet the same year, and
    subsequently reprinted.

17 An attempt was made shortly before Flodden by Garret
    Mor, earl of Kildare and Hugh O'Donnell of Tyrconnel
    to persuade a not-unsympathetic James IV to support
    an Irish rebellion against England, and the Scots
    duly attacked Carrickfergus. Lamb's reference does
    not apply accurately to these events, and he may be
    thinking of a subsequent attempt to revive this
    short-lived alliance.

James, persawand þe Kyng of Ingland stomocate,
nocht tretable to continuew amite with his nephew,
schew þat his maistir, Kyng of Scotland, within
ten ȝeiris befor sindre tymes had mair opportunitie
5   to mak novatioun a contra his vncle, as quhon Guid
Scalco, send be Charlis Imperatoure for tendir
luif and confideratioun with þe Scottis kyng, incontinent eftir þe Lundoun Perliament declarit þat
Elizabeth, begottin vpone Anna, to be repute
10 apperand air of Ingland, ȝour kyngis vthir wyif,
Quene Katherine of Spane, and Lady Marie, hir
dochtir, being þan on lyif. Als þe sam Leirmonth
schew how ȝour kyngis nephew wes nocht facill quhen
þe nobill bluid of Ingland wes persequutit, nor
15 quhen þe insurrectioun of þe commonis raiss last.
Also Leirmonth schew þat the Kyng of Scotland culd
nocht be brokin fra his vncle be solistatioun of þe
Erle of Kildare and Odoneill in Irland. Gif the
Kyng of Scotland omittit all thir occurrantis and
20 oportuniteis, quhy sould he now, haifand na concurrantis, walkin besines a contra his vncle, quha
neuer a quheit movit at ocht þat Leirmonth said,
nor movit for proximitie of bluid, with sindre
gratuiteis of his nephew, bot commandit þe Duik of
25 Norphok suld prepair his army be all diligence and
pas fordwart in Scotland.

Guid man of Sion

Now becaus we entir in þe toun of Rowane I think
_____
19 of Scotland interlin. MS.

24 Cf. <u>Declaration</u>, sig. c i^v (p. 200):

... as Maryan a Scot writing that storye in
those dayes graunteth, confesseth and testifieth
the same ...

best þat ȝow baith, guid freindis, continew ferder
commonyng in this mater till we returne to our
vaiage ..... Becaus I traist þat euerilk ane of ws

f. 361^r hes done / his besines weill, and becaus we ar now

5   enterit agane in our jornay to Pareiss, latt ws
entir oure auld commonyng of Inglis just weir with
Scotland.

Inglis.

ȝow, nichtbour Scott, apperit at oure entering in
Rowane for to reput all þe forsaidis causis of weir

10   of litill valour: quhat can ȝow say to þe anciant
demand of superioritie that Ingland hes vpone
Scotland, recognoscit successiuelie be þe Scottis
kyng be deidis, werdis, actis and writtingis continewalie without interruptioun or at þe leist

15   intermissioun?

Scott.

As to þe fyift causs, of þe Ingland kyngis superioritie in Scotland, ȝour buik vpone þe declaratioun
of þis weir makis mair diligence and labour for to
deduce þat pretendit superiorite fra þe first

20   growing of þe auld roulkis in þis greit ile þan it
dois pruif þe samyn attentiklie, nochtwithstanding
þe sam buik labouris to induce thre maneris of
probatioun vpone the superioritie, as be historijs,
instrumentis and registreis.   Bot a thing I mer-

25   well, quhy ȝour buik specifeis alanerlie bot ane

_____
3 ane interlin. MS.

historiciane, callit Mariane, Scottis writtare, for
to pruif þe first homage, maid þe ix. hundreth ʒeir
of Christ, and for to pruif all þe vthir homagis
fra þat tym to þe homage maid j^{m} v^{c} ʒeir of Christ?

5   I intend to impung euerie ane of þir pretendit
homagis be Polidor, ʒour awin liturate, autentik
historiciane, and gife neid beis I sall impung
be ane cuning, grave and diligent ancient air
callit Hectour Boece, our trew historiciane.

10   First of all, it apperit weill þat Kyng Henrie þe
Aucht and his counsell report þe foure before-namit
causis nocht sufficient to perswade the facill
Inglis pepill that he movit just weir aganis his
nephieu bot gife he had addit þis new-forgit
15   superiorite.   Neboure, pleiss ʒe þat I ansuer at
anis to all the discurse of homagis contenit in
ʒour buik, or þat I ansuer to every homage be itself?

Inglis.

No, in faith, I lik nocht þat ʒow ansuer attonis,
20   for þan ʒow will mak bot ane refusale and deming
to all!

First, quhat sayis ʒow to the probabilite and lik-
nes of sic superiorite from þe first habitatioun
of Albioun for þe bettir administratioun of justice
amangis ruid peopill; as twa or ma of ane estait

---

20 mak _interlin._ MS.

5 Cf. <u>Declaration</u>, sig. b iv^v-c i^r (p. 199):

For as it is probable and lykely that for the
better administration of iustyce amonges rude
people, two or mo of one astate mighte be rulers
in one countrie vnite as this Isle is: so is it
probable and likely that in the beginnyng it was
so ordred for auoydinge discention, that there
shuld be one superiour in right, of whom the
said astates should depende. According whervnto
we rede how Brutus, of whom the realme than
callyd Brytayn toke fyrst that name (being before
that tyme inhabited with gyauntes, people without
order or ciuilitie) had thre sonnes, Locrine,
Albanact, and Camber, and determinyng to haue the
whole Isle within the Occean sea to be after
gouerned by them thre, appoynted Albanact to rule
that nowe is called Scotland, Camber the parties
of Wales, and Locrine that nowe is called Englande:
vnto whom as beinge the elder sonne, the other
two brothers shuld do homage, recognisynge and
knowleagyng hym as theyr superior.

mycht be reullaris in ane cuntrey vnit as þis ile
is, so it is probable and liklie þat in þe begyning
it wes sa ordourit for avoding of dissentioun þat

f. 361ᵛ   þair suld be ane superioure, in rycht of quhom / þe

5   said twa or ma estatis suld depend, as did begin in
þe monarche of Bruit, and syn the haill administratioun devydit in Locrin, eldest superiour
brothir, also in Albanat and Cambir, ӡongar
brethering.

Scott.

10   Nichtbour, ӡow and ӡour Kyng Henry þe viij. in þe
Declaratioun of þis weir sayis þat þe administratioun of þat land is best quharin þair is twa
or ma reularis of ane estait, as Locrin, Cambir
and Albanat, maid be Brutus, first monarche of þis

15   ile.

Nebour, I do speir quhar be now Camberis posterite?
Quha reulis his part of this ile, now callit
Vallia?   I traist ӡe will ansuer þat Vallia is
vnit to Locrinis part, now callit Anglia: suyth ӡe

20   say.   Than I speir be quhat titill, quhiddir be
mariage, subdewit or fre surrendering?   Bot I
traist þat Vallia is vnit to þe Inglis crown as þe
vthir sax Saxonis realmes was, and as ӡe now desyr
Scotland.

---

4   quhom repeated MS.
5   ma   MS. has reullaris of ane estait as locrin,
       deleted by scribe.

6   Cf. <u>Epistle</u>, sig. a iv^r (p. 239):

> And though he were a straungier to bothe, what
> would he thynke more mete, than if it wer
> possible one kyngdome be made in rule, whiche
> is one in language, and not to be diuided in
> rulers, whiche is all one in Countrey.

18   See Caesar, <u>De bello gallico</u>, v, 12-13.

Inglis.

The kyngis maieste dois posseid nor will posseid no
thing bot be just titill.

Scott.

Kyng Henry þe viij. sayis in his Declaratioun of
þis p<u>rese</u>nt weir that twa or ma reullaris in this
5   ile is necesser for bettir administratioun of
justice, bot Edward, Duik of Summersett in his
Exhortatioun for vnioun of Scotland with Ingland
sayis be mony allegationis þat ane kyng, ane reulare in this land is best. At quhithir of þir twa
10   opinionis will ȝow abyde, þat I may ansuer conformelie bot to þis ȝo<u>u</u>r p<u>rese</u>nt opinioun? Ȝow say
as did begin in Brutus tyme: nebour, ȝe most nedis
stabill þis ground of Brutus monarchie, þaireftir
consequenter ȝo<u>u</u>r probabilite of twa or ma reullaris
15   will appeir mair apparent. Heireftir gife it be
sperit quhen /in/ quhat leid was þis historie
writtin and be quhom, quhat salbe ȝour ans<u>ue</u>r?

For Julius Cesar, ane diligent, inquisitiue writtar, haifand vnder his gyding threttie or fourtie
20   men xiiij. or xv. ȝeiris continewalie, eftir his
vesiyng tuyss þe partis quhar þat Loundoun is situ-
ate a fiftie ȝeir afor þe natiuitie of Christ, wald
haif als reddalie haif writtin þe origin of þis
ile, the first inhabitoris, reullaris, gife ony

---

4   Cf. Tacitus, <u>Agricola</u>, 21 (ed. W. Peterson /London
    191<u>4</u>/, p. 206:

        Iam vero principum filios liberalibus artibus eru-
        dire, et ingenia Britannorum studiis Gallorum ante-
        ferre, ut qui modo linguam Romanam abnuebant, elo-
        quentiam concupiscerent.

11 Cf. Gildas, <u>De excidio Britannie</u>, 4 (ed. Hugh Williams
    /London 189<u>9</u>/, p. 18:

        ... quantum tamen potuero, non tam ex scriptis
        patriæ scriptorumve monimentis, quippe quæ, vel si
        qua fuerint, aut ignibus hostium exusta aut civium
        exilii classe longius deportata non compareant ...

memorie or historie had bene þat tym amangis þe
Brittanis, as he did diserine þe peopillis maneris,
þe longitude and latitude of þe samyn Britane.

Cornelius Tacitus sayis þat þe Brittanis childring
5   begouth to leir literatoure and Romanis ciuiliteis
quhen Julius Agricola gydit Britane vnder þe
Romanis; giff literatour begouth in þis ile about
lxxxx. ʒeir eftir þe natiuitie of Christ, it
f. 362^r apperis þair wes litill /or titter na literatour
10   befor þat tym. Also, þe v^c lxxx scor ʒeir eftir þe
birth of Christ, Gildas Britan sayis þair culd na
historie buikis be fund of þe sowth partis of
Britan in þis tyme. Heirfore, þat is for þe want
of literatour and memorie of anciant dedis befor
15   Julius Cesar and also before Gildas, in quhais tym
and na sonare begouth the oppressioun of Britane
befor ane peopill (heir I excep þe Romanis conqueist). It man be said þat Brutus monarchie and
his thre sonnis is als vncertane as þe origin of
20   all vthir nationis except alanerlie þe origin of
Isralite peopill be provitioun of God, and also of
Inglis origin, quharof þe authoris maner is weill
knawin to all þame þat redis þe Inglis historijs.
Bot gife ʒe, nebour, will say þat Britane was in
25   Brutus and his thre sonnis tyme eftir the Dilugit,
vpone sic a ground ʒe may devyd þis ile and beild
sic probabilitie as ʒe lyk ymagin.

10/14 Also ..... in þis tyme. Added in margin
      MS.

1   Cf. <u>Declaration</u>, sig. c i^{r-v} (p. 199):

  ... but some authors, as Anthonius Sabellicus
  amonges other diligently enserchyng, what he
  might truely write of all Europe, and the
  Ilandes adioyninge, ouer and besides that whiche
  he writeth of the nature, maners, and conditions
  of the Scottis, whiche who so lyst to rede, shal
  fynde to haue bene the very same in tymes paste,
  that we finde them nowe at this present, he
  calleth Scotlande part of Englande, which is
  agreable to the diuision aforesayd, beinge in
  dede as in the lande contynuall without
  separation of the sea, so also by homage and
  fealtie vnite vnto the same ...

The reference is to the Italian historian, Marcus
Antonius Coccius Sabellicus, whose unflattering
account of the Scots in his <u>Enneades</u>, X, v, <u>Opera</u>
<u>omnia</u> (3 vols, J. Hervagius: Basel 1560), II, col.
943, begins 'Scotia suprema Angliæ pars est ad
septentrionem ...'

17 For the sixteenth-century background to this view of
Sabellico's reliability, see above, Introduction, p.
xxiii.

Inglis.

Sayis no<u>ch</u>t Antonius Sabilicus þat Scotland is ane
part of Ingland, quhilk is aggreable to þe diuisi-
oun afore be me said, being in deid as in þe land
co<u>n</u>tinewalie without separatioun of þe sey, also
5   be homage <u>and</u> fealtie vnit?

Scott.

Be this ʒour argument, Asia, Europia and Aphrica is
vnit to ʒo<u>u</u>r kyng be homage and fealtie, becaus
France is in Europe and ʒo<u>u</u>r kyng dois repute him-
self kyng of France, and thai sam thre partis of þe
10 w<u>a</u>rald ar co<u>n</u>tinewall in land wi<u>th</u>out separatioun
of þe sey. Bot nebour, ʒour buik culd no<u>ch</u>t haif
notit a passage in all Sabillikis workis for mair
ignorance and infamitie of þe auctor; bot it is
mair to be me<u>r</u>valit on þe makar of þis ʒo<u>u</u>r buik,
15 and also one the authorisate Counsell of Ingland,
þat allegit sic ane discriptioun of Scotland,
Sabilicus Italiane, quha as can be provin hes errit
baith in historie and discriptioun of landis about
his awin durris in Italie.

20 Nichtbour, can ony man in Ingland, beand no<u>ch</u>t
blind in witt, mynd and body (as, alace, ʒe be now),
say þat Scotland is or was evir a part of Ingland
mair nor France ane part of Spanʒe; quharof gif ʒe
pruif no<u>ch</u>t be pr<u>eten</u>dit homagis bettir þan Sabili-
25 cus previs Scotland ane part of Ingland, ʒo<u>u</u>r fyre
is bot ane smuke and ʒo<u>u</u>r kyng and Counsell hes

5   Lamb here introduces Polydore Vergil's <u>Anglica
    Historia</u>, upon which much of his subsequent argument
    will depend. For the evidence that it was the 1534
    edition that he used, see Introduction, p
    Denys Hay's comparison of the 1534 and 1546 editions
    (<u>Polydore Vergil</u> /Oxford 1952/, pp. 187-98) reveals
    numerous small differences, but few involve re-
    traction of statements made in the earlier edition,
    and there is nothing to confirm Lamb's statement.
    But Leland (1544) and Bale (1548) had attacked
    Polydore for his criticism of favourite English
    historical myths, ibid., pp. 157-9.

8   Richard Smith, Regius Professor of Divinity at
    Oxford, was the author of a number of theological
    works, and had disputed at Oxford with both Ridley
    and Peter Martyr. His <u>Godly and Faythefull Re-
    tractation</u> (R. Wolfe: London 1547) was the published
    version of his recantation (15 May 1547) of opinions
    expounded in <u>A Brief Treatise of the Apostles
    Traditions</u> and <u>The Assertion and Defence of the
    Sacramente of the Aulter</u>; although it denies a
    number of Catholic doctrines, its recantation is
    less sweeping than Lamb suggests. Smith was soon
    in further trouble, and fled to Scotland on his way
    to the Continent; it is therefore possible that
    Lamb's reference to his fortunes is based upon
    personal acquaintance. On Smith's career, see

21 Cf. <u>Declaration</u>, sig. c i^{v} (p. 200):

        ... we shal begyn at the yere of our lord Dccc ...
        Edwarde the fyrst before the conquest, sonne to
        Alured kyng of Englande, had vnder his dominioun
        and obedience the king of Scottis. And here it
        is to be noted, that this matier was so notorious
        and manifest, as Maryan a Scot writing that story
        in those dayes, graunteth confesseth and testifieth

authorisate ane freuole buik and enterit ane inextingguabill, iniust weir for sobir causis.

That Scotland is nocht nor neuir was ane part of
Ingland I call to witnessing all gentill and cuning
5   men of Ingland, and als Polidor in his first, thrid
and in all his buikis of Inglis historijs, to þe
first prent; for I heir ʒe maid þe puir man call
agane mony trew thingis, as ʒe did Doctour Smytht
quhen ʒe drew a recantatioun for him and causit
10   ʒour lordis to threatin him to deith. He denyit
þat Christ wes cuming, denyit þe sacrifice of þe
Mess, and pronuncit to be lauchfull for temporale
f. 362ᵛ men to possess spirituale / promotioun: this ʒe
outhir compellit him to do, or ellis to presoun.
15   So strang is ʒour argumentis of þe court of
Ingland!

Inglis.

I will pas oure þe auld historiis and begin þe ixᶜ
ʒeir eftir Christis natiuitie, quhen Kyng Edwart þe
First befoir þe Conqueist begouth to regne, quha
20   had vnder his dominioun the kyng of Scottis, quhilk
continewit xxiij. ʒeiris. This previt Marian, a
Scottis writtare.

Scottis.

Now I se ʒe condiscend to perticulare homagis; bot

---

5   in his MS. adds buikis, cancelled by scribe.
8   Doctour Smytht added later MS.
13 spirituale repeated MS.

10   Marianus Scotus (1028-1082/3) was an Irish monk who
     was successively at Cologne, Fulda, Würzburg and,
     from 1069, Mainz, having left Ireland at the age of
     28.

13   For the coronation of Edward in 901 see Polydore
     Vergil, <u>Angl. Hist.</u>, p. 105; his defeat of King
     Constantine is recorded p. 109.

26   The form of the names given by Polydore Vergil (p.
     110) is Sithricus, Analaptus and Gotthofredus.

28   Cf. Boece, fol. 223^{v}.

becaus þis mater is greit and wechtie it mone be
seriuslie provin, and na substantiall poynt of
probatioun omittit be ȝow and siclyk na sub-
stantiale poynt of impugnatioun omittit be me.

5   Bot nebour, þis ȝour first homage is generale,
quharin nothir Scottis kyngis name nor place nor
day of homage-making is specifeit; and as to ȝour
pruif of homage be Marian, a Scottis writtare, we
Scottis-men knawis nocht quhithir he wrett in

10 Caldaic or Hebreac leid, for he is na mair in
Scotland than Matussalem writing, or Heli, Enoch
and sic.

Now neboure, heir quhat ȝour Polidor in his sext
buik writtis: Kyng Edwart wes crownit in þe ix^{c} and

15 ane ȝeir of Christ, he vincust Constantine, Scottis
kyng, sua allargeit the marchis of his awin realme
that exceptit Scotland he obtenit þe haill impyre
of þe ile, howbeit at þat tyme þair wes sum
dominioun on Northumberland vnder þe Danis.

20 Nebour, in the forsaid passage of Polidour is said
except Scotland, and also na mentioun is maid of
homage or superiorite of ȝour Kyng Edwardis tyme
vpone Scotland. Forder, it is weill knawin þat
Northumberland wes ay as ȝitt þe last and northmest

25 schirefdome of Ingland and nerrast Scotland, and
bounding fra ȝork to Berriwik: mairoure, in þis
Kyng Edwardis tyme in þe sam Northumberland rang
Schiddric Dane, haifand Edith, or as Boece sayis

---

5 ȝour interlin. MS.

7 Cf. <u>Angl. Hist</u>., p. 108.

9 Cf. <u>Angl. Hist</u>., p. 107:
    Per hunc demum modum, is rex fines regni ita
    propagauit, ut iam preter Scotiam, totius insulae
    imperium obtineret.

Beatrice, þe sam Kyng Edwardis dochtir in mariage,
of quham wes borne Analeph and Gothfred. Thir twa
wes chesit furth of Northumberland be Athilstane,
þair awin mothir brothir. Swa sum dominioun in
5   Northumberland beand vnder þe Danis be Polidoris
awin wordis, Scotland wes nocht subdewit.

This Kyng Edward decessit þe ix^c xxv. ʒeir of oure
Lord, eftir he had regnit xxiiij. ʒeiris, sayis
Polidor. This Polidor exceptis speciale Scotland
10   fra þe Inglis impire without distructioun of
proprietie or superioritie, and also exceptit a
f. 363^r part of Northum- / berland fra þe Kyng Edwardis
dominioun, as ʒe may se in his sext buik of þe
Inglis historiis. Now, guid man of Sione, ʒe se
15   how Kyng Henry þe viij. and his Counsell hes laid
and stabillit lapidem angularem of þir pretendit
homagis; bot how he beildis heirupone, I pray ʒow
attend!

Inglis.

The ix^c xxiij. ʒeir, Kyng Athilstane be battell
20   conquerit Scotland, maid ane Constantine kyng to
reule and governe vnder him.

Scottis.

Nebour, quhat wald ʒe think gife I said to ʒow þat
Robert Huid had conquerit Italie and maid Romulus

---

12 Northum- repeated MS.
15 hes MS. adds his couns, subsequently deleted.

2   Cf. <u>Angl. Hist</u>., p. 109:

Sed Constantinum ita uictum, in uerba sua iurare
iussit, id quod ille fecit, quo sibi per eum
liceret, in posterum tempus, uita atque regno uti,
frui.   Idem aliquot deinde Scotorum reges fecisse
traduntur, quod recentiores eorum scriptores
multis argumentis disputant.   Nos uero tale quid
agere, nostri muneris minime esse ducimus, cum
historia rerum gestarum narratio, non item con-
tentio sit, qui proinde ea quae annales Anglicani
antiquissimi loquuntur, nobis scribendi constitu-
imus, quo sine ulla cuius piam populi offensione,
inchoatum opus perficiamus.   Ita a principio
praefari libet, ut non sit deinceps quisquam omnium, qui ab historico de quauis re praeteritis
seculis gesta, officium iudicis requirat,
flagitet, desideret.

14   Cf. <u>Declaration</u>, sig. c i^v (p. 200):

... at whyche tyme Athelstaine succeded in the
crowne of Englande, and hauyng by battayle conquerit Scotlande, he made one Constantine kynge
of that partie, to rule and gouerne the countrye
of Scotlande vnder hym, adding this princely
woord, That it was more honour to hym to make a
kyng, than to be a kyng.

28   Cf. <u>Angl. Hist</u>., p. 146:

... Northumbros demum in fidem recepit, Atque ita
primus Anglorum regum totius Angliae imperium
obtinuit.

kyng of Rome? Bot Polidor in his saxt buik sayis:
Sed Athelstanus Constantinum ita victum in sua
verba jurare jussit quo sibi liceret per eum im-
posterum vita atque regno vti, et frui. Idem
5   deinde aliquot Scotorum regis fecisse traduntur,
quod recentiores eorum scriptores multis argumentis
disputant: nos vero tale quid agere, nostri muneris
minime esse ducimus. /Ita/ a principio prefari
libet, vt non sit deinceps quisque omnium, qui ab
10   /historico/ de quauis re preteritis seculis gesta,
officium judicis requirat, flagitet, desideret.

Nebour, ȝe may reid in Polidor that this Kyng
Edwart decessit in the ix^c and xxv. ȝeir of our
Lord, and ȝour buik vpone this weris declaratioun
15   sayis Athilstane conquerit Scotland and maid
Constantine kyng þairof þe ix^c xxiij. ȝeir of
Christ; and sua tua ȝeiris Athilstane or him-self
wes kyng of Ingland, and or Kyng Edward wes deid,
conqueist Scotland and maid Constantine kyng of
20   Scotland. And suyth ȝe say, it is a princelie
thing, a man to conquess a realme and mak his
inime a kyng þairof or he be a kyng him-self. And
albeit ȝour buik of þis weris declaratioun and
Polidoris calcalatioun micht be aggreit, ȝit
25   Polidour myndit be his wordis of Latine forsaid
that it is difficile to ane historiane for to
affirme sic auld wechtie dedis as homagis for
certane. Ferder, he sayis in his viij. buik of

8 Ita MS. sta
10 historico MS. historio

13 Cf. <u>Declaration</u>, sig. c ii^{r} (p. 200):

   xxiiij. yeres after that, whyche was the yere of
   our lorde D cccc xlvij, Eldred kynge our progenitour, Athelstains brother, toke homage of
   Irise, then king of Scottis.

Inglis historijs thus: <u>Athilstanus Northumbriam</u>
<u>demum in fidem recepit, atque ita primus Anglorum</u>
<u>regum totius Anglie imperium obtinuit</u>. Heir is
no<u>ch</u>t said þat <u>Athilstanus recepit Scotos</u> nor
5   <u>totius Britanie imperium</u>; be quhilk word <u>Britanie</u>
wes þan and also now is co<u>n</u>tenit bayt<u>h</u> Ingland and
Scotland.

Als it is doutsum ama<u>n</u>gis the Inglis historiante
quhithir þis allegit subdewing of Scotland and
10   making of kyng þairof was þe act of Athilstane or
of Edmu<u>n</u>dus his brother. This aboue is provin in
Polidorus vi. and viij. buik of Inglis historiis.

Inglis.

Tuenty four ȝeiris eftir, did no<u>ch</u>t Kyng Eldred of
Ingland resaif homage of Irische, than kyng of
15   Scottis, þe ȝeir of o<u>ur</u> Lord ix. hundret<u>h</u> xlvij.
ȝeiris?

f. 363^v   Scot.

Nichboure, quhen ȝe find in Polidour, ȝo<u>ur</u> awin
principale historiane, or in ouris, Hector Boece,
that þair wes ane kyng of Scotland at þat tyme
20   callit Irische, than sall I prepair me to impruife
the sam. It apperit þat ȝo<u>ur</u> makar of þe buik
vpone þe weris declaratioun fand þis homage in sum
Irische buik! Also, Polidor writtis in his sext

_____

12 Polidorus <u>MS. adds</u> vij, <u>subsequently deleted</u>.

7   See above, 73/4-5.

buik þat to þe forsaid Constantine, Kyng of Scotland succedit Macolme, Induloch, Duf, Culen, Chened
and Constantine, ilk eftir vthir, to þe crown of
Scotland. Amang all þe forsaid ⌐namis⌐ ʒe find
5 nocht ane Scottis kyng callit Irische. Ferder,
gife ony Inglis-man wald wse for probatioun þir
wordis in þe saxt buik of Polidor, Item aliquot
reges Scotorum fecisse traduntur, this is generale
and sufficient probatioun of ix. or x. homagis!
10 This is provin becaus Polidor makis na ferder
mentioun of þe Scottis in his vj., vij. or viiij.
buik.

Inglis.

Threttie ʒeir eftir, quhilk wes ix^c lxxvij. ʒeir
of Christ, did nocht Edgarus, Kyng of Ingland tak
15 homage of Kynnald, Kyng of Scotland? And xl.
ʒeiris eftir, quhilk wes j^m xvij. ʒeiris of Christ,
siclik our Kyng Knoot resauit of ʒour Kyng
Macolme; and alsua xxix. ʒeiris eftir, quhilk wes
j^m lvj. ʒeiris of Christ, Sanct Edward oure kyng
20 vincust Kyng Macolme and conquerit Scotland and
gaif it to his sone Macolme, quha maid homage
þaireftir.

Scottis.

Nebour, ʒe pruife waiklie, or rather na thing at
all, þe last pretendit homagis. Also, I say þat

---

4 namis MS. manis

1   The complicated list of dates of pre-Conquest kings
    which follows, drawn from Angl. Hist., pp. 114-40,
    is principally intended to show that the year of the
    claimed homage to Edgar (977) is impossible. On
    this point Lamb is quite correct: Edgar died on 8
    July 975 (cf. Angl. Hist., p. 117). But either he
    or his scribe is becoming confused, since the date
    of death his given as 977 at 79/5 and as 975 at
    79/15-16.

23 Again Lamb is right; but the reference in the Decla-
    ration must be to Kenneth II (971-995).

outher ȝour buik of weir or Polidor hes skoupit in
calculing of Kyng Edgaris ringne, for Polidor in
his sext buik sayis Edger wes crownit kyng of
Ingland þe ix^c lix. ȝeir of Christ and decessit
5   about þe ix^c lxxvij. ȝeir, at quhilk tyme wes
Edward crownit and þe ix^c lxvij. ȝeir slane be þe
wayis of Alfred, slane be his step-moder. Also
Polidor sayis þat Knook, Kyng of Denmark wes
crownit kyng of Ingland þe j^m xvij. ȝeir of Christ
10 and decessit þe j^m xxxvij., and þat Edward Confessour wes crownit kyng of Ingland þe j^m xliij.
ȝeir of Christ and decessit j^m lxv. ȝeir. Gife
Edgar resauit þis homage ix^c lxxvij. ȝeir of
Christ, as ȝour buik of þis weris Declaratioun
15 sayis, and gife þe sam Edgar deceissit þe ix^c
lxxv., as Polidor writis, necessarlie followis þat
þe executouris of Kyng Edgaris testament resauit
this homage twa ȝeiris eftir Edgaris deceiss.
Also, þis conquering of Scotland be Sanct Edwart
20 þe Confessour, it apperis þat it wes be miracle,
for nother in Polidor nor in Boece is red þat he
maid ony weir aganis Scotland.

f. 364^r Also, he nor the Scottis historijs makis na mentioun of sic a Scottis kyng as Kynald; forder,
25 apperandlie Polidor wald nocht haif omittit nouther weir nor homage done to Knook and to Edward,
kyngis of Ingland, gife ony had bene maid; and swa
þe homage of Kynnald and of twa Scottis kyngis
callit Macolmus is sufficientlie improvin.

7   Cf. <u>Angl. Hist</u>., p. 154.

21   Cf. Hector Boece, <u>Scotorum Historiae</u> (J. Badius
     Ascensius: Paris 1527), f. 267^r:

     Wilhelmus nondum bello satiatus, filium suum
     Robertum cum maioribus quam antea vnquam copiis
     in Northumbros mittit; sed is ad Tinam fluuium
     sedens nullam rem gessit memoria dignam, tantum
     Nouum castrum ab hostibus poene directum
     reparauit, domumque rediit. Tandem vero pax

Inglis.

Ellevin ʒeiris eftir, in þe ʒeir of our Lord j^m
lxviij., William þe Conqueror accomptit na perfite
conqueist vntill he had elikwyiss subdewit þe
Scottis and maid þe said Malcolme, Kyng of Scottis
5   to do him homage as his superiour be conqueiss of
Ingland.

Scottis.

ʒour Polidor sayis: <u>Pax data Scoto sub ea lege vt</u>
<u>in Guilielmj verba iuraret</u>.

Nebour, it is verisimile þat a nobill, vaillieant,
10   vertius, lovit kyng be his people all his dayis as
þis Kyng Malcolme of Scotland wald haue subdewit
him-self, his fre realme without straik or schak of
swerd, for Polidor makis na mentioun of battell,
alanerlie bot of Inglis mennis incursionis, becaus
15   our Kyng Macolme recuilʒeit þe Conquerouris
rebellis.

Als, thocht ʒour Conqueror had win ane battell <u>a</u>
<u>contra</u> þe Scottis, as he neuer did, ʒitt I can
rekin ʒow tuenty and ma battellis fochin <u>and</u> neuer
20   þe realme of Scotland þairthrow subdewit nor
superiorite demandit. Tharfor Boece in his tuelf
buik of Scottis historijs sayis þat Guiliame þe
Conquerour send Robert, his eldest sone, with ane
greit army aganis Macolme kyng, bot maid pece that
25   sa mekill of Northumberland lay betuix Tueid,
Cumber and Staimor suld remane with Macolme, and

4   On the so-called Rere Cross of Stanmore, cf. the
    draft version of Fordoun's Book V, <u>Chronica Gentis
    Scotorum</u>, ed. W.F. Skene (2 vols, Edinburgh 1871-2),
    i, 433-4, and Andrew of Wyntoun, <u>Original Chronicle</u>,
    ed. F.J. Amours (STS, 6 vols, Edinburgh 1903-14), iv,
    398-401; in both these sources, its erection is
    attributed to the reigns of David I and Stephen. But
    Lamb is following Boece, fol. 267^r, who places it in
    the reigns of Malcolm and William.

15 So the <u>Declaration</u>, sig. c ii^{r-v} (p. 200).

25 Cf. <u>Declaration</u>, sig. c ii^v (p. 200):

    xxv yeres after that, whiche was the yere of
    our Lorde mxciii. the sayde Malcolme dyd homage

þat at þe marchis was erectit ane croce: on þe ane
syd of þat ilk croce was þe image of þe Conqueror,
on þe vthir syd þe image of Kyng Macolme, and
þairfor it wes callit þe Re Croce. Also, ȝour

5   Conqueror causit þis sam Robert incontinent eftir
beild New-castell as þe vtmaist on of Ingland
marchis towart Scotland.

Mairattoure, countrey-man, I speir at ȝow, and also
at Polidor, quhat war þe wordis quharupone ȝour

10 Conqueror maid sa nobill a kyng as Macolme to
sueir, and also in quhat ȝeir and in quhat place;
for it is our generale writtin and also interpretit
for to subdew ane realme be þir wordis: jurauit in
verba. Bot becaus ȝour buik of weir culd nocht

15 pruif vthirwyiss þis homage, in it is addit þir
wordis: Kyng Malcome did homage to William Conqueror as superiour be conqueist of Ingland; so
apperit þat þe mynd quha conquesis Ingland, to him
f. 364ᵛ necessarlie most þe Scottis kyng mak homage. / Be

20 þe sam reasoun, þe Scottis kyngis maid homage to
the Saxonis, to þe Danis, to þe Normannis, and
also to all vthir nationis þat subdewit Ingland;
quhilk is no moir trewth nor quhyt is blak. My
foir-saying Polidor and ȝour buik of weir provis.

Inglis.

25 Tuentie-fyue ȝeiris eftir, in þe ȝeir of our Lord
jᵐ nyntie and thre, þe said Malcolme did homage to

---

19 homage repeated MS.

and fealtie to William Rufus, sonne to the sayd
William Conquerour: and yet after that was for his
offences and demerites deposed, and his sonne
substytute in his place, who lykewyse fayled in
his duetye, and therfore was ordeyned in that
astate by the sayd William Rufus, Edgare brother
to the laste Malcolme, and sonne to the fyrste,
who dyd his homage and fealtie accordingely.

20 Cf. Angl. Hist., p. 167:

... ac tunc Robertum ducem nomine regis, opera &
consilio Edgari militis Normani id temporis ex-
ulis, qui sub Scoto stipendium faciebat, cum
Malcolmo qui cum ualidissimo exercitu prope suos
fines in armis stabat, operiens Anglorum aduentum, pacem composuisse, ac nonulla loca ex
pactione Scoto restituta, quae ille rege primo
Gulielmo, in Anglia possedisset.

William Ruffis, and for his demeritis wes deposit
and his sone substitute in his place, quha in lyk-
wyiss falit in his dewitey; and þairfor Edgar,
brothir to þe last Malcolm and son to þe first
5   Malcolme, was ordanit in þat royale estait be Kyng
Ruffus.

Scott.

Nichbour, heir ȝe most be remembrit of ȝour buik
of weir sayis Kyng Edwart the Confessour vincust
and deposit þe first Malcolme and gaif Scotland to
10   Malcolme þe Secund and his sone Macolme þe Thrid
fra þe crowne of Scotland, and in þat estait he
ordanit Edgar, þe last Malcolmeis brothir and þe
first Macolmes sone.

Heir is to be notit ane mervalus thing, that ony
15   man sall haif twa fatheris, or ellis þe sam a man
salbe his brotheris father, as þis Edgar was Macolmes þe First sone and succedit to his brothir
Macolme þe Thrid, quha with his fader Macolme þe
Secund was deposit be ȝour Kyng Ruffis.

20   Forder, Polidor in his tent buik writtis mani-
festlie contra þis ȝour allegeance, saying thus:
Willelmus Ruffus Robertum fratrem ducem Normanie
quando Macolmus cum validissimo exercitu prope
suos fines in armis stabat, expectans regis Ruffi
25   et Anglorum aduentum, pacem /composuisse/, ac
nonulla loca ex pactione Scoto restituta, que ille
rege primo Villelmo in Anglia possidisset. Nouther

25 composuisse MS. compusuisse

15 Neither the scene of this homage nor a reference to
    the authority of the witnesses is in fact mentioned in
    the Declaration, and it is not easy to see why Lamb,
    who is usually meticulous in his representation of the
    English case, should have added this assertion.

19 For the death of Macbeth in 1061 and the accession of
    Malcolm III, cf. Boece, fol. 264^v. But Macbeth was
    actually killed in 1057 (although his stepson Lulach
    then reigned for a year until he too was killed in
    battle), and Malcolm controlled southern Scotland from
    1054; see A.A.M. Duncan, Scotland: The Making of the
    Kingdom (Edinburgh 1975), p. 100.

27 Angl. Hist., p. 169: 'Alneuichum'; Boece, fol. 269^r:
    'Alwick'. Malcolm III was killed near Alnwick on 13
    November 1093.

at þis componyng of peace nor eftir vnto þe deceiss
of Macolme, Polidor makis mentioun of ony homage;
bot he writis planlie be þe said wordis þat þe said
Macolme possedit landis in Ingland in þe Conquer-
5 ouris tyme, quhilkis landis was restorit be ȝour
Kyng Williame Ruffis, as ȝe may heir.

Nichtboure, heir is to be notit a greit obedience
of Scottis kingis to Ingland, þat sufferit þame-
selffis be sa oft deponit without straik or schak
10 of swerd or ony just caus etc!

Sembleablie is to be notit a greit clemence of
Ingland, quhilk restorit so mony Scottis kyngis;
bot sic is the humanitie of godlines off Lundoun
court now þat it wald nocht peraduentour vse sic
15 clemencie thir dayis! ȝour buik of weir referris
þe probatioun of þir depositionis and restitu-
tionis of kyngis to þe nobill men that wes present
at þat tyme in þe Cokfeild besyd Westminster; bot,
f. 365ʳ nebour, oure Boece, historiane, / writis þat þis
20 first Macolme wes nocht crownit kyng of Scotland
quhill the jᵐ lxj. ȝeir of Christ, and swa his
sone Macolme maid homage to Sanct Edward fyve
ȝeiris or his fader wes kyng of Scotland! Als þis
sam Malcolme continewalie and peceablie rang kyng
25 of Scotland quhill his deceiss, and swa he was
nocht deposit fra þe crown bot deceissit kyng at
Anmeroik in his army, as Polidor verefeis, jᵐ

---

3 planlie *interlin. MS.*
19 historiane *repeated MS.*

9 Cf. <u>Declaration</u>, sig. c ii^V (p. 201):

   vij. yeres after that, whiche was in the yere of
   our lorde MC. the sayd Edgar kynge of Scottis,
   dyd **homage** to Henry the fyrste, our progenitour.

12 Cf. <u>Angl. Hist</u>., p. 169:

   Scoti mortuo Malcolmo, Dunaldum eius fratrem,
   illius nominis tertium regem creant, quem Dun-
   canus filius nothus ipsius Malcolmi auxilio regis
   Gulielmi Rufi, apud quem iuuenis obses est, qui
   bifarium diuisus, hinc Dunaldum, illinc Duncanum
   petebat regem ...

lxxxxvij. ʒeir of Christ, and in þe tent ʒeir of
Kyng Ruffis regne. Sen þe Scottis kyng Macolme
quha wes in ʒour kyng Etheldred and Suenoyis tym,
we reid and findis alanerlie bot Kyng Macolme Can-
5   mor in ʒour Conqueroris tyme and Malcolme Virgin
in Kyng Henryis the Secundis tyme; swa apperis
nocht sa mony kyngis Macolmis deposit and restorit
as ʒour buik of weir dois mentioun.

Inglis.

Sevin ʒeiris eftir þe last homage, the sam Kyng
10   Edgar did homage to Kyng Henry the First, jᵐ jᶜ
ʒeir of Christ.

Scottis.

It is contenit in Polidoris tent ⌐buik⌐ þat
Donald, Malcolmis brothir, was immediatlie crownit
Scottis kyng, and, he eiectit be a Scottis fac-
15   tioun, wes crownit Kyng Duncan, þe sam Macolmes
bastard sone, quha also wes eiectit be ane vthir
Scottis factioun; for it is said þat þe vse wes in
Scotland in tha dayis þat þe Scottis kyng being
ane minor, þe abillast and nerrast potent agnet
20   rang and gydit þe realme.

It apperis þat ʒour minʒeonis of þe court wes mair
circumspect to compleiss Kyng Henrie last in
imagining and seiking of þir homagis than thai war
to seik and proif the ground and trew veritie of

---

12 buik om. MS.

11 Cf. <u>Declaration</u>, sig. c ii^v (p. 201):

> xxxvij. yere after that, Dauid kyng of Scottis
> did homage to Matilde the Emperatrice, as
> daughter and heyre to Henry the fyrst.

23 Polydore Vergil gives the date of Stephen's coronation
    in <u>Angl. Hist</u>., p. 194, and the length of his reign,
    ibid., p. 206.

þe samyn etc.

Attoure, als sone as þis Kyng Henrie was crownit
kyng of Ingland he marijt Matild, þis sam Edgaris
sistir, and swa it apperit þat Kyng Henrie wald
5 noᴄht haif chargit his guid-brothir with sic ane
vnpleisand thirlage; bot gife ȝe will say þat Kyng
Edgar thoᴄht a greit honour to mak homage at þe
wedding of his sistir, forder Polidor makis na
mentioun þat ony contraversie raiss betuix thir
10 twa guid-brethir, or þat Edgar maid ony homage.

f. 365ᵛ   Inglis.

Threttie-sevin ȝeir eftir, did noᴄht ȝour Kyng
Dauid obedience to Mattild þe Imperatrice, in þe
ȝeir of Christ jᵐ jᶜ xxxvij. ȝeir?

                      Scottis.

It apperis þat ȝour buik will say þat Kyng Dauid
15 maid this homage be reasoun of þe Impire; and gife
þair be ony vthir reasoun, than I say that þis
forsaid ȝeiris homage can noᴄht stand with þe
verite: quhilkis Kyng Stephane wes crownit kyng of
Ingland at Westminster vpone Christmess Day jᵐ jᶜ
20 xxxvi. ȝeir, and one þe xxv. day of October, the
ȝeir of Christ jᵐ jᶜ liiij. ȝeir, this Stephane
decessit eftir he had regnit xix. ȝeiris, xj.
monethis and vij. dayis, as Polidor writtis in his
xij. buik, and eftir Stephane immediatlie wes
25 crownit kyng of Ingland Henrie the Secund, þis

9 Cf. <u>Declaration</u>, sig. c ii^v (p. 201):

   ... After whiche Dauids deathe, whiche ensued
   shortly after, the sonne of the sayd Dauid made
   homage to the said kyng Steuen.

21 <u>Angl. Hist</u>., p. 206.

samyn Matildis sone; and swa þis forsaid homage
was maid to Matild nouthir befor nor behind Ste-
phanis ringne, or ellis 30ur buik hes necligentlie
insertit þis obedience.

5   This my calculatioun 3e will find in Polidor, bot
gife 3e wald say þat Matild wes crownit quene and
also Stephane Kyng rangne in Ingland bayth at a
tyme?

Inglis.

Eftir quhilk Dauidis deith, his sone maid homage
10   to Kyng Stephane.

Scottis

Neboure, how was this sone of Dauidis namit, quhen
or quhare was he crownit kyng of Scotland, and also
quhen or quhar maid he þis omage to 30ur Kyng
Stephane? Heir 30wr buik of weris declaratioun
15   hes craftalie slippit þe interspace betuix Kyng
Dauidis homage and his sonnis homage, and als hes
slippit the 3eir of Christ, for to eschew þe impugnatioun. Also þe samyn buik hes fallin in ane
slumber of errour, saying þat Kyng Dauidis sone
20   maid homage to Kyng Stephane.

Polidor in his xij. buik sayis þat Kyng Dauid decessit laitlie befor Stephane, and to Dauid succedit Macolme, his nepote of his sone Henry, quha
wes maid Erle of Huntingtoun be Kyng Stephane and
25   did homage to Stephane. Tharfore, as Polidor

1   Cf. <u>Angl</u>. <u>Hist</u>., p. 208:

    ... deinde in Northumbriam profectus, eam quoque
prouinciam totam recuperauit, quam Dauid rex
Scotorum sibi donatam a matre eius Mathilde cuius
partes secutus fuerat, primum tenuerat una cum
Cumbria comitatu iampridem capto de rege Stephano,
& dein Macolmus nepos qui ei successerat, id
temporis possidebat: sed ut ne uideretur iniquus,
aut beneficiorum immemor, permisit eum comitatum
Hunthyngtonam retinere, quem iampridem Stephanus,
uti supra diximus, Henrico filio Dauid dono
dederat, qui ob id, conceptis uerbis etiam iusiurandum sibi daret.

19   Cf. <u>Declaration</u>, sig. c ii^{v} (p. 201):

    xiiij. yeres after that, whiche was in the yere of
our lorde MCL. William king of Scottes, and Dauid
his brother, with al the nobles of Scotland made
homage to Henry the secondes sonne, with a
reseruation of theyr duetie to Henry the second
his father.

sayis in his xiij. buik, <u>vnam Northumbream Dauid</u>
<u>rex Scotorum sibi donatam ab Henrici Secundi Anglie</u>
<u>matre Mathilde cuius partes sequutus fuerat, pri-</u>

f. 366^r   <u>mum tenuerat vnacum Cumbria comi- / tatu iampridem</u>

5   <u>/c̄apt͟o/ de rege Stephano, et deinde Macolmus nepos</u>
<u>qui Dauidi successerat, id temporis possidebat.</u>
<u>Sed Henricus Secundus vt ne videretur iniquus, aut</u>
<u>beneficiorum immemor, permisit eum comitatum Hung-</u>
<u>tinthonam retinere, quem iampridem Stephanus, vti</u>

10   <u>supra diximus, Henrico filio Dauid dono dederat,</u>
<u>qui Henricus ob id, conceptis verbis etiam ius-</u>
<u>iurandum sibi daret.</u>

Heir may ʒe se ane manifest contradictioun betuix
Polidor and ʒou͟r buik, quha sayis þat Dauidis sone

15   succedit kyng in Scotland, and Polidor sayis þat
Macolme, Dauidis nepote, succedit kyng. This nedis
na vther pruife than Polidor in his tuelf and
threttein buik.

Inglis.

The fourtene ʒeiris eftir, quhilk wes j^m j^c l. ʒeir

20   of Christ, — ʒow Scottis be to laith for to knawlege ʒou͟r errour — did no͟cht ʒou͟r Kyng William
and Dauid his brothir homage, and all þe nobillis
of Scotland, to oure Kyng Henryis Secundis sone in
þe ʒeir of ou͟r Lord j^m j^c l. ʒeir?

---

4 comi- <u>repeated MS</u>.
5 capto <u>MS</u>. rapto

1   Lamb is, of course, taking no account in the argument
    which follows of the succession dispute following the
    death of Henry I, in which David II himself played a
    part. The account in the <u>Declaration</u> of this confused
    period is much more lucid than he is prepared to con-
    cede.

26   Robert Gaguin, <u>De Francorum gestis</u> (Jean Petit: Paris
     1507), fol. 94^v; <u>Angl. Hist.</u>, p. 205.

Scottis.

The homage Maidtilde j^m j^c xxxvij. ʒeiris, and it
maid to Stephane, and als þis homage maid j^m j^c l.
ʒeiris, man be repute ane mervalus thing; for gife
Polidoris calculing of ʒeiris be just, saying that

5   þe kyng Stephane was crownit þe j^m j^c xxxvj. ʒeir
of Christ and decessit þe j^m j^c liiij. ʒeiris,
necessarlie follovis þat Mathild Imperatrice,
Stephane, Henrie þe Secund and his sone Henrie
rang in Ingland all at ane tyme, that is betuix þe

10 j^m j^c xxxvj. and to þe j^m j^c liiij. ʒeir, within
þe quhilk space of þe tyme ʒour buik of weir will
say that Dauid, Kyng of Scottis, his sone syn,
William and Dauid his brothir maid homage to
Matild, Stephane, Henry þe Secund, and to his sone

15 Henry, kyngis of Ingland. Swa ʒour kyngis buik
hes slumberit, or ellis Polidor hes errit in calculatioun; bot I beleif suirlie that þe authorite
and wisdome of Ingland wald nocht haif sufferit sa
evident ane errour in þair principall cronicle.

20 Nichtbour, apperis ʒow laik memorie: said I nocht
laitlie ʒour Polidor writis how þat to Macolme,
Kyng of Scottis succedit William his brothir,
quhom ʒour buik of weir sayis maid homage to Kyng
Henryis Secund sone in þe j^m j^c l. ʒeir of Christ?

25 Howbeit as Polidor sayis, Stephane wes on lyif þe
j^m j^c liiij. ʒeiris. Als, be Gaguine, Franche
historiane, and be Polidor, Kyng Henry þe Secund

---

8 þe Secund ... Henrie added in margin MS.

22 Cf. <u>Declaration</u>, sig. c ii^{v}-iii^{r} (p. 201):

    xxv. yeres after that, which was in the yere of our
    lord MCLXXV. William kyng of Scotlande, after moche
    rebellion and resistence, accordyng to their natur-
    all inclination, kyng Henry the second, than being
    in Normandy, William then kyng of Scottis know-
    ledged fynally his errour, and made his peace and
    composition, confirmed with his great seale, and
    the seales of the Nobilitie of Scotland, makynge
    therwith his homage and fealtie.

marijt no<u>ch</u>t Alenor, the heretrice of Aquitane,

quhill eftir Kyng Lodovik of France returnit fra

f. 366^{v} Jherusalem, the quhilk returny<u>ng</u> / wes in þe ȝeir

of Christ j^{m} j^{c} lij. ȝeiris, and þaireftir Kyng

5   Lowis repudiat þe said Alenor vpone quhome Henrie

þe Thrid wes begottin, quhomto thai allege Kyng

William maid homage in þe j^{m} j^{c} l. ȝeir. And swa

gife Polidorus calculing of ȝeiris be trew, Wil-

liam maid þis <u>pretendit</u> homage to Kyng Henrye the

10   Secundis sone twa ȝeir or he wes borne, that is to

say, twa ȝeir or Alenor was marijt one Henry þe

Secund, quhilk wes about þe j^{m} j^{c} lij. ȝeiris of

Christ, and also four ȝeiris or Kyng Stephane

decessit, quhilk wes þe j^{m} j^{c} liiij. ȝeiris of

15   Christ.

For þis calculatioun I call to pruif Polidor and

the Frenche historiane Gaguin and all vther just

croniclis. Now, guid man of Sione, quhat juge ȝe

of þir homagis quhilk the vncle, Kyng of Ingland,

20   allegis ane just caus for to mak weir one þe

Scottis?

Inglis.

Tuenty-five ȝeiris eftir, in þe ȝeir of o<u>ur</u> Lord

j^{m} j^{c} lxxv., can ȝow deny þat William ȝo<u>ur</u> kyng

did homage to Henry þe Secund?

---

3   retu<u>r</u>nyng <u>repeated MS.</u>

4   j^{m} j^{c} <u>MS. continues</u> lx, <u>deleted by scribe.</u>

16 Cf. <u>Declaration</u>, sig. c iii^r (p. 201):

   Within xv. yeres after that, which was the yere of
   our lorde MCLXXXX. the sayd Wylliam kynge of
   Scottes came to our citie of Canturburie, and there
   dyd homage to our noble progenytour kynge Richard
   the fyrste.

20 Cf. <u>Angl. Hist.</u>, p. 240:

   Fecit idem Guilielmus rex Scotiae ... Ac Scotus

Scottis.

Being anis ane errour in calculing admittit, force
that sam errour mone continew or ellis incress,
quhilk cleirlie improvis this homage. Bot ȝitt it
is lyk þat þe Lundowne court wes one sleip quhen
5   it authorisate þe buik vpone þis weir, for sup-
porting that þe calculatioun in it war just, ȝitt
in it is said þat Kyng William maid homage in þe
ȝeir of Christ j^m j^c l. to Kyng Henry, sone of
Henry þe Secundis sone, and eftir in it /̄is̄/ said
10   þat Kyng William maid homage to Kyng Henry þe
Secundis selfe in the j^m j^c lxxv. ȝeir: be þis
apperis ane manifest preposter ordour by custum of
all vther cuntreis, that the fader succedis to his
awin sone, as apperis that Henry the Secund suc-
15   cedit to Henry, his awin sone!

Inglis.

Within xv. ȝeiris eftir, this sam Kyng William come
to þe cietie of Cantirberry and þair did homage to
oure Kyng Richard þe First, in þe ȝeir of our Lord
j^m j^c lxxx. ȝeiris.

Scott.

20   Sic as Polidor, ȝour historiane writis thus: Fecit

---

8   MS. has Henry the Secundis sone And efter in
        it said þat Kyng William maid homage to Kyng
        Henry þe Secundis selfe in þe j^m j^c
        deleted by scribe.
9   is om. MS.

interim uel rebus suis mature consuluit, quippe
qui Castellum Puellarum, Beruicum, Roxburgum, &
Sterlingum redemit a rege, quae loca paucis ante
annis, Henrico eius patri loco pignoris dederat.

8   Cf. Declaration, sig. c iii^{r} (p. 201):

xiiij. yeres after that, the sayde William did
homage to our progenitour kynge John, vpon a hyll
besides Lincoln .....

12 Cf. Angl. Hist., pp. 261-2:

Venit sub idem tempus Londinium, salutatum Ioan-
nem regem Gulielmus rex Scotorum, iusiurandumque
dedisse fertur.

idem Willelmus rex Scotie ac Scotus interim vel
rebus suis mature consuluit, quippe qui Castellum
Puellarum, Beruicum, Roxburgum, Sterlingum redemit
a rege Richardo, loco pignoris paucis annis ante
5   data. Gife þis Kyng William past in Ingland,
schaw þe causs quhy and makis na mentioun of
homage: Polidor verefeis þis.

f. 367^r In/g/lis.

Within xiiij. ȝeiris eftir, did nocht þe sam Kyng
William homage to our Kyng Jhone vpone þe hill
10   beside Lincolme, in þe ȝeir of Christ j^m ij^c and
four ȝeiris of Christ?

                    Scott.

I reid in ȝour Polidoris xv. buik thus: venit sub
idem tempus Londinium /salutatum/ Johannem regem
Villelmus rex Scotorum, jusiurandum dedisse fertur.
15   Gife be þir wordis of Polidor mycht be inducit ony
homage, ȝit be þir sam wordis apperis cleirlie
nother his place and tyme of homage aggreis with
ȝour buik, quhilk twa thingis is specialie requirit for þe solempnizing of ane greit acte sic
20   as homage.

Also, howbeit Kyng William had cumin to Lundoun
fertur dedisse iusiurandum, heir Polidor schawis
nocht nor affirmis certane for quhat caus þat Kyng

---

13 salutatum MS. salutatem
21 had cumin MS. had cuming had cumin

8 Cf. <u>Declaration</u>, sig. c iii^r (p. 201):

    xxvi. yeres after that, whiche was in the yere of
our lord MCCXVI. Alexandre kyng of Scottes maryed
Margaret, the doughter of our progenitour Henry the
thyrde, at our citie of Yorke, in the feast of
Christmas: at which tyme the said Alexandre dyd his
homage to our sayde progenitour . . . . .

William swear.

Forder, þis ȝour buik makis þis Kyng William haue
maid four homagis: the first to ȝour Kyng Henry þe
Secundis sone, syn to Kyng Henryis þe Secund selff,
5   the thrid to Kyng Richard, the ferd to Kyng Jhone
at Lyncolme, and as apperis he maid þe fyft in
Londoun, as Polidor wryttis.

Inglis.

Within xxvi. ȝeiris eftir, ȝour Kyng Alexander
marijt Mergaret, dochtir of oure Kyng Henrie þe
10   Thride, and maid his homage to þe sam Henry in þe
ȝeir of Christ j^m ij^c and xvj.

Scott.

Nichtbour, þis pretendit homage suld be reknit
maid in þe ȝeir of Christ j^m ij^c and xxx., becaus
ȝour buik sayis that Kyng William maid his homage
15   in þe j^m j^c l. ȝeir, tharfor þe nixt homage within
xxv. ȝeiris was maid in Normundy, syn ane homage
at Cantirberre within xv. ȝeir, eftir quhilk
followit þe homage of Lyncolme within xiiij. ȝeiris, and now tuenty-sax ȝeiris of þis present
20   homage of Kyng Alexander at ȝork; the quhilk for
particulare numeris togiddir with j^m j^c l. extendis till j^m ij^c xxx. ȝeiris, quhilk tym man be
said þat Alexander maid þis his first homage.
Reid ȝour buik of weir and ȝe will find ȝour kyng
25   and Counsell and nocht þe prentare haue falit in

2 The phrase 'Cum priuilegio ad imprimendum solum', indicating royal authority for the printer's work,
   occurs with Berthelet's colophon at the end of the
   1542 edition of the Declaration.

3 For the two coronations of Henry III, cf. Angl. Hist.,
   pp. 285, 289; the marriage of Joanna to Alexander II
   of Scotland is noted, ibid., p. 290.

18 Cf. Declaration, sig. c iii^{r-v} (p. 201):

    ... betwene the homage made by the sayde Alexander
    kyng of Scottes, and the homage done by Alexander,
    sonne to the sayde kyng of Scottes, to Edwarde the
    fyrste at his coronation at Westmester, there was
    about fyfty yeres, at whiche tyme the sayde Alex-
    ander kynge of Scottes repaired to the sayde
    feast of coronation, there did his duetie as is
    afore sayde.

authorising of sic ane tretie prentit at Lundoun
<u>cum regali preuilegio</u>.

f. 367^V Forder, ʒo<u>u</u>r Polidor sayis þat þis ʒo<u>u</u>r Kyng Henrye wes first coronat the xvij. day of November in
5   þe ʒeir of God j^m ij^c and xvij., and þaireftir he
sayis þat þe sam Kyng Henry wes crownit at Westminster in þe ʒeir of Christ j^m ij^c and xx. and
gaif Joanna his sistir to Kyng Alex<u>ande</u>r o<u>u</u>r kyng
in mariage. Swa gife ʒe, nebour, will follow
10   Pollidoris calculing, Kyng Alex<u>ande</u>r maid þis
first p<u>rete</u>ndit homage a ʒeir or Henrie þe Thrid
wes first crownit, and swa ʒo<u>u</u>r authorite hes
falit, bayth in þe ʒeir of Christ and in þe heid
of Kyng Henryis coronatioun.

15   Nebour, reid ʒo<u>u</u>r awin buik vpone þis weir and
also ʒo<u>u</u>r awin Polidor for vereficatioun of þis my
forsaid allegeance.

Inglis.

Fiftie ʒeiris eftir Alexanderis homage maid in
ʒork, his sone Kyng Alex<u>ande</u>r maid homage to Ed-
20   ward þe First eftir þe Conqueist, at his coronatioun in Westminster in þe ʒeir of Christ j^m ij^c
lxxvj.

Scott.

Nichtbour, ʒo<u>u</u>r Polidor writis in his xvij. buik

---

3   sayis <u>interlin</u>. MS.
4   coronat <u>interlin</u>. MS.

1   Polydore Vergil actually gives the date of the coro-
    nation of Edward I as 1274, Henry III having died the
    previous year, _Angl. Hist._, pp. 315-6. Lamb is in
    danger of becoming lost in a welter of dates, many of
    them inaccurate and all of them in Roman numerals; and
    his point about a seven-year gap does not seem to make
    sense.

9   Lamb is misled by a peculiarity of the calculations in
    the _Declaration_: the homage of William the Lion to
    Richard I is dated 1190 (see above, 101/16), and that
    to John was 'xiiii yeres after that', i.e. 1204. But
    the marriage of Alexander II to the daughter of Henry
    III, 'xxvi yeres after that', is counted from 1190 not
    1204, and is stated to have taken place in 1216. Lamb
    simply adds all the intervals together, and gets 122
    years instead of the correct figure of 130. In the
    end, however, he seems to arrive at 1280 (fourteen
    years after 1266), a date which, although it is wrong
    historically, makes some sense given Lamb's original
    assumptions.

23 Cf. Quintilian, _De institutione oratoria_, 4.2.91:

        verumque est illud, quod vulgo dicitur, mendacem
        memorem esse oportere.

    The phrase was proverbial in the sixteenth century,
    and is quoted by Polydore Vergil, _Angl. Hist._, p. 177,
    referring to the reign of Edgar.

24 Cf. _Declaration_, sig. c iii^v (p. 201):

        Within xxviii. yeres after that, which was the yere
        of our lorde MCCLXXXII John Baliol kynge of Scottes

of historijs that Edward þe First wes crownit in
þe j^m ij^c lxxiij. ʒeir of Christ, swa þis homage
is no<u>ch</u>t trew, or ellis it wes maid or Kyng Edward wes crownit vij. ʒeir. Alswa, þis coronatioun
5   and <u>pret</u>endit homage was maid in þe j^m ij^c lxxij.
ʒeir of Christ giff þe particulare spacis of
homagis be trewlie collectit and gife eu<u>er</u>y ane of
þame lestit so lang as ʒo<u>ur</u> buik of weir reportis,
becaus ʒo<u>ur</u> buik sayis this: the homage maid þe
10   j^m j^c l. ʒeir of Christ lestit xxv. ʒeiris, the
nixt indurit xv. ʒeiris, the thrid xiiij., the ferd
xxvj., the fyft indurit l. ʒeiris, quhilk /̄parti-
culare̲7 spacis togiddir collectit makis j^c and
xxij. ʒeiris, the quhilk collectioun with þe said
15   j^m j^c and l. extendis to j^m ij^c lxxij. ʒeiris. Be
þis hale nu<u>m</u>mer necessarlie Edwardis coronatioun
and þis <u>pret</u>endit homage wes maid xiiij. ʒeiris
eftir þe j^m ij^c lxvj. /̄ʒei<u>r</u>7 of Christ. Swa ʒo<u>ur</u>
weir-buik nothir aggreis with it-self nor with
20   Polidor in this Edwardis coronatioun: sa followis
þis last Alexanderis homage improvin. This Alex-
<u>ander</u> marijt Mergaret, dochtir to Kyng Henrie þe
Thrid, <u>decet mendacem esse memoriam</u>.

Inglis.

Within xxviii. ʒeiris eftir þe homage maid last at

----

2   Christ   <u>interlin</u>. MS.
5   homage   <u>interlin</u>. MS.
12   particulare   <u>MS</u>. particularlie
18   ʒeir   <u>om</u>. MS.
21   Alexanderis   <u>MS. has</u> coronatioun, <u>cancelled</u>.

made homage and fealtie to the sayde kynge Edwarde
the fyrst, our progenitour.

23 Lamb here seems to echo Aristotle, <u>Poetics</u>, 7, which
    he may, of course, have read in the Latin version,
    translated by William van Moerbeke in the thirteenth
    century: Totum autem est habens principium medium et
    finem (ed. Erse Valgimigli, <u>Aristoteles Latinus</u>,
    xxxiii /Bruges/Paris 195<u>3</u>/, p. 11).

25 What follows is a fairly accurate summary of Polydore

Westminster, I sall say vnto ʒow a thing veray
cleir: did nocht Jhone Ballioll ʒour kyng homage
and fealtie to Kyng Edward þe First, in þe j^{m} ij^{c}
lxxxij. ʒeiris of Christ etc.?

f. 368^{r} Scottis.

5   Nebour, þis homage is impugnate be ʒour-selfe and
    ʒour buikis calculatioun, for addand xxviii. to
    j^{m} ij^{c} lxxx. as ʒe mone necessarlie calcull sen þe
    homage maid in þe j^{m} j^{c} l. ʒeir of Christ, ʒe sall
    find j^{m} iij^{c} ʒeiris of Christ, and swa þis homage
10 was maid xviij. ʒeiris eftir þe j^{m} ij^{c} lxxxij.
    ʒeiris of Christ; and consequenter, be refewing of
    þir twa last homagis, all þe precedent and also
    all þe following homagis most necessarlie decase
    for laik of stabillisment of dow tyme.

15 Forther, admittand þe calculatioun of ʒour buik,
    be proponyng of þis Balliollis homage ʒe procure
    ane greit dishonour bayth to ʒour Kyng Edward and
    also to ʒour awin Inglis natioun quhen ʒe sett
    furth sa abstinatlie a manifest iniust actioun be
20 ʒour awin procedingis, þe quhilk procedingis ʒe
    compell ws to oppin.

    I pray ʒow, countray-man, reid ʒour awin Polidor
    in his xvij. buik and ʒe will find the begyning,
    þe myd and fyn of þis Balliolis homage trewlie
25 declarit, in þe quhilk xvij. buik Polidor sayis
    þat þe princis of Scotland, seand þair realme

───────
3 Edward interlin. MS.

Vergil's account, <u>Angl. Hist</u>., p. 323.

27 For the story of the Roman arbitration in a dispute
    between the people of Ardea and Aricia (not Aretum!),
    by which the Romans awarded the contested lands to
    themselves, see Livy, III, 71-2.

destitude of a direct liniell kyng and dreiding
ciuile weir to ryiss amangis þame-selffis gife
thai had chosin ane haifand na richt to þe crown
of Scotland, the richt þairof pertenyng to þe
5 childring quhilk come of Erle Dauid of Huntingtoun
thre dochteris, ȝour Kyng Edward being ane wyiss,
potent prince as ony was in tha dayis, quha in
case þe nobillis of Scotland had repellit þe
Bruce, þe Ballioll and þe Haisting, or admittit
10 ony of þame to þe crown of Scotland, Edward wald
haue concurrit to with ony of þe thre compitetaris
þat had bene repellit fra þe Scottis crown, quhomwith he had likit best for vsurpatioun of Scotland,
as þe Scottis lordis supponit.

15 Heirfore, the lordis of Scotland referrit to ȝour
Kyng Edward quhone þe discussioun of þe Scottis
crownis richt with consent of þe Bruce, Ballioll
and Haisting as to ane newtrale, just, prudent
prince; bot he, lik as God had putt evidentlie in-
20 to his hand be ane vngodlie way the perfite ending
of x^c ȝeiris strife betuix þe twa realmis, and lik
as God had send to him specialie þe monarchie and
impire of þis haill ile of Britane, thinkand nocht
onlie tyme cumit for to mak þe superioritie of
25 Scotland his awin bot also þe selfe propirtie,
ȝour Kyng Edward procedit in discussing of þe thre
richtis as did þe peopill of Rome betuix þe Ar-
deatis and þe Aretinis.

---

8 þe nobillis of Scotland _interlin. MS._
26 þe _interlin. MS._

5 Cf. <u>Angl. Hist.</u>, p. 324:

   Rex Edwardus postquam in concilio cum suis principibus de re Scotica agitauerat, oratoribus respondit,
   se perinde populi Scotici ac Anglici libertatem,
   rempublicam suo studio, consilio, patrocinio con-
   seruaturum: sed cum interregnum esset, & olim Scoti
   reges fidem saepissime suis maioribus obligassent,
   uelle speciatim a Scotis principibus conceptis
   uerbis iusiurandum sibi dari, ut Scotiæ terræ
   domino, atque cunctas regni arces in suam potestatem tradi, ac tum demum se daturum operam regi
   creando. Legati accepto responso, mandata Edwardi
   ad principes sedulo detulerunt, quibus et si petitio visa est nedum aspera, at parum iusta, ut
   Anglus non arbitrum regis creandi, sed dominum
   Scotiæ ageret, attamen quia inter se iam dissidebant, morem regi gesserunt.

17 Cf. <u>Angl. Hist.</u>, p. 324:

   ... ipsique Ioanni regni Scotiæ possessionem sua
   autoritate confirmauit. Ioannes per hunc modum rex
   factus, primum omnium in uerba Edouardi iurat: dein
   in Scotiam reuersus, eo ipso die qui diuo Andreæ
   sacer est, & apud eam gentem maxime celebris, magno
   cum totius populi gaudio coronatur.

f. 368^v I pray ȝow, nichtbour, attend: Polidor in his xvij.
buik writis this eftir þe Scottis lordis had re-
queistit be þair ambaxatouris Kyng Edward for to
accept þe discussioun of þir forsaid thre richtis:

5   Rex Edwardus respondit legatis Scotorum se velle
speciatim a Scotis principibus conceptis verbis
jusiurandum sibi dari, vt Scotie terre domino atque cunctas regni arces in suam potestatem tradi,
ac tum demum se daturum /operam/ regi creando;

10   legati Scotorum accepto responso, mandata Edwardi
ad principes suos sedulo detulerunt, quibus et si
petitio visa nedum aspera ac parum justa, vt
Anglus non arbitrum regis creandi, sed dominum
Scotie /ageret/, attamen principes Scoti quia inter

15   se dissidebant morem regi gesserunt.

Nebour, þis the prelude and acceptatioun of þis
honest jugement! Syn eftir sayis Polidor: Ipsius
Johanni Balliolo regni Scotie possessionem sua
authoritate confirmauit Edwardus; Johannes vero

20   per hunc modum rex factus, primum omnium in verba
Edwardi jurat, deinde in /Scotiam/ reuersus cum
magno populi gaudio coronatur. Nebour, heir is þe
just ground of þe Balliolis allegit homage, þe
quhilkis nedis na impugnatioun becaus it is sa

25   honest, sa just, and sa princelie a jugement.

---

9   operam MS. operaui
11 et si MS. has petito vi, cancelled by scribe.
14 ageret MS. ageretis
21 Scotiam MS. Scotie

1 Cf. <u>Declaration</u>, sig. c iii^v (p. 202):

   ... For within xliiii. yere after, whiche was the
   yere of our lorde MCCCXXVI. Edwarde Baliol, after
   a great victory in Scotlande agaynst thother
   faction, and enioyenge the crowne of Scotland, made
   homage to our progenitour Edwarde the thyrde.

9 For the death of Edward II in 1327, see <u>Angl. Hist.</u>,
   p. 354. Dealing with the events of the following year
   Polydore Vergil indicates that Robert I was still
   alive. The error in the <u>Declaration</u> is almost certainly a misprint caused by the omission of an 'X',
   since Balliol was in effective control of Scotland in
   1336.

17 Cf. <u>Angl. Hist.</u>, p. 358.

Inglis.

Eftir xliiij. ʒeiris, did nocht Edward Ballioll,
eftir greit victorie enioying þe crown of Scotland,
homage to oure Kyng Edward the Thrid, þe ʒeir of
Christ j^m iij^c xxvi.?

Scottis.

5   Be the forsaid calculing of þe induring of þe pretendit homagis maid sen the j^m j^c l. ʒeir of
Christ, this Balliolis pretendit homage suld fall
in þe j^m iij^c lij. ʒeir, for Polidor sayis that
Kyng Edward þe Secund decessit þe j^m ij^c xxxvij.
10 ʒeiris of Christ, also he sayis þat Robert Bruce
remanit kyng of Scottis quhill eftir þe ʒeir of
Christ j^m iij^c xxviij. ʒeir, sa þis allegit victorie and joysance of þe Scottis crown be Edward
Ballioll and homage maid be him the j^m iij^c xxvj.
15 ʒeiris apperandlie hes bene amangis þe ladyis of
Lundoun.

Also, Polidor sayis þat ʒour Kyng Edward the Thrid,
in þe j^m iij^c xxxij.ʒeir of Christ helping Edward
Ballioll to þe Scottis crowne, maid weir one
20 Dauid, Kyng of Scotland, of x. ʒeiris of aige and
haifand weddit Joanna, his full sistir, the quhilk
Dauid was immediatlie crownit kyng of Scotland
eftir Kyng Robert Bruce his fader.

f. 369^r This may ʒe se cleirlie, þat Ballioll for help and

---

24 may corrected in MS. from man.

8 Cf. <u>Declaration</u>, sig. c iii^V (p. 202):

> And, xx. yeres after that, which was in the yere of
> our lorde, MCCCXLVI, Dauid Bruse, who was euer in
> the contrary faction, did neuerthelesse in the
> title of the crowne of Scotland, wherof he was then
> in possession, make homage to our sayde progenitour
> Edwarde the thyrde.

support to be maid to him-selff be Kyng Edward, he
maid þis pretendit homage, bot þis Edward Ballioll
for þis sam homage-making wes schortlie deposit
fra þe crown of Scotland, and levit eftir as ane
5   prevat man in France vpone his Frenche sein3eouris;
and neuer ane þat come of him succedit to þe crown
of Scotland vnto þis day.

Inglis.

Tuentie 3eiris eftir, quhilk wes j^m iij^c xlvj. 3eir
of Christ, 3ow can nocht deny þat Kyng Dauid Bruce
10   maid homage to Kyng Edward þe Thrid.

Scottis.

Nichtboure, þis homage wes maid xxviij. 3eiris
later, or ellis the induring of þe forsaidis homagis ar nocht trewlie collectit nor calculat be
3our Kyng Henrie þe viij. sen þe j^m j^c l. 3eir of
15   Christ, quhilk spacis of homagis collectit makis
j^m iij^c xxi. 3eir of Christ; and swa þis homage is
to mak or ellis wes maid xxviij. 3eiris later þan
3e mene. 3e allege mony homagis, bot neuer ane
lauchfull nor valeur.

20   Nichtbour, 3e sall nocht reid in na buik ane greitar humanite þan it quhilk 3our thre Kyng Edwardis
did to Scotland; for Kyng Edward þe First a contra
Robert Bruce and Haisting, competitouris, adiugit
be his decreit arbitrale the crown of Scotland
25   for to pertene to Jhone Ballioll, the quhilk

20 Cf. <u>Angl. Hist.</u>, p. 359:

   Caeterum autores habeo, aliam huiusce belli causam
   fuisse, & eam omnino ueriorem, qui tradunt Edouar-
   dum regem ideo bellum fecisse Dauid regi, quod
   ille pernegasset more maiorum, in eius uerba
   iurare, ut ne per id Anglum terræ Scotiæ dominum
   se agnouisse fateretur. Sic Edouardus recepto
   oppido, ac alijs postea locis de Scoto captis,
   Baliolum quem sibi iureiurando obligauerat, præ-
   fecit .....

Ballioll, Edward þe First, eftir greit lang continewall weir wes furth of Scotland eiectit be
Robert Bruce, than Kyng Edward þe Secund renuncit
all superiorite and maid pece, and Edward the
5   Thrid maid pece and gaiff Joanna his full sistir
to Dauid, Kyng Robertis sone. Bot sone eftir, he
expellit bayth Joanna his sistir and Dauid, of ten
ʒeiris of aige, and he compellit þame to pass into France be support maid for þe crownyng of Ed-
10   ward Ballioll kyng of Scotland, and þane causit þe
sam Ballioll for to resingne to him baith propirtie
and superiorite of Scotland and maid him-self be
crownit kyng þairof. Bot within quhene ʒeiris,
this Kyng Edward þe Thrid wes eiectit furth of
15   Scotland be the nobillis, and brocht þair Kyng
Dauid with Joanna his wyf fra France, of quhome
ʒour Kyng Edward þe Thrid resauit þis pretendit
homage befor his passing in France.

Polidorus, cullerand this humane deid of Edward
20   the Thrid, sayis: Tradunt Edwardum tertium ideo
bellum fecisse Dauidi regi, quod ille pernegasset
more maiorum, in eius verba iurare, vt ne per id
Anglum terre Scotie /dominum/ se /agnouisse/ fateretur. Sic Edwardus tertius rex Anglorum recepto
25   Beruik, / et aliis postea locis de Scoto captis,
f. 369ᵛ
quem sibi iureiurando obligauerat, /prefecit/.
Edward Ballioll, and þis Kyng Edward supportit
Edward Ballioll be schippis and men to attene to

23   dominum MS. dominium; agnouisse MS. agneuisse
25   Beruik repeated MS.; locis interlin. MS.
26   prefecit MS. perfecit

3   This point about English restraint is twice made in
    the Declaration, at the beginning where reference is
    made to James V 'being then in the myserable age of
    tender youthe (sig. a ii^v), and more explicitly in the
    final paragraphs, in which the recent failure of the
    English to pursue their supremacy is attributed to the
    minority of the Scottish king (sig. d iii^{r-v}).

8   Cf. Declaration, sig. c iii^v-iv^r (p. 202):

    Within ix. yeres after, this Edward the thyrd, to
    chastise the infidelitie of the Scottis, made warre
    agaynst them: where after great victories, Edwarde
    Balliol hauyng the iust and ryght title to the
    realme of Scotlande, surrendred clerely the same to
    our said progenitour at the towne of Rokysbrough in
    Scotlande: where our said progenitour accepted the
    same, and than caused hym selfe to be crowned kynge
    of Scotlande, and for a tyme enterteygned it, and
    enioyed it, as very proprietary & owner of the
    realme, as on thone parte by confiscation acquyred,
    and on the other parte by free wyll surrendred vnto
    hym.

crowne of Scotland <u>a contra</u> his leag maid with this
Dauid Bruce, his awin guid-brothir and a pupill at
þat tyme. Bot Kyng Henrie þe viij. sayis mair
guidlie, that he wald nouther seik homage nor con-
5   queist of Scotland in þe tyme of þe Scottis kyngis
minorite; bot his deid was vthir-wayiss, for he did
weir twyiss on his nepote, þan beand minor.

Inglis.

Within nyn ʒeiris eftir, quhilk ⌊w̅es̲⌋ j^m iij^c lv.
ʒeir of Christ, Edward Ballioll eftir greit vic-
10   torijs haifand þe just richt and titill to þe
realme of Scotland, surrenderand cleirlie the
samy<u>n</u> to oure kyng Edward the Thrid, quha acceptit
þe samy<u>n</u> and þan causit him-selff to be crownit
kyng of Scotland, and for a tyme intertenijt and
15   joyit þe sam as veray proprietare awnare of þat
realme, as þe on part be confiscatioun acquirit
and on þe vthir be fre will surrenderit vnto him.

Scott.

Nichtboure, for to incress ʒo<u>ur</u> buik of weir ʒe
returne agane to Edward Ballioll, bot quha ma than
20   Inglismen sayis þat Edward Ballioll had the just
richt titill of Scotland? Bot admitting þat Edward Ballioll had þe just richt, nebour, I speir
at ʒow quha surrenderit þis richt titill, and be
quhat ordour, quhat tyme and in quhat place? Also,

---

8   wes <u>om</u>. <u>MS.</u>

19 Cf. <u>Declaration</u>, sig. c iv^r (p. 202):

> And yet Henry the V. for recouery of his ryght in
> France, commaunded the kyng of Scottis to attende
> vpon hym in that iourney.

> Lamb's scepticism notwithstanding, the English claim
> was accurate on this point: James I was commanded by
> Henry V to participate in the French campaigns of
> 1420 and 1421.

22 Immediately before the statement quoted above, the
    <u>Declaration</u> remarks that during the reigns of Richard
    II and Henry IV 'the Scottis had some leisure to play
    their vagues, and folowe their accustomed manier'.

nebour, realmes vsis nocht to be surrenderit as
betuix þe byar and þe sellar of horss and ky.
Also, admitting ȝour superiorite, quhat parteis
was callit to þis process and sentence of con-
5 fiscatioun of Scotlandis propriete; also quhen and
quhar wes þis sentence gevin? I think weill þis
is Kyng Edwardis þe Thridis proceding and sentence,
conforme to his humane dedis a contra his guid-
brothir of ten ȝeiris agit, a contra his awin leag
10 and band.

Also nichbour, giffe þis surrendering and confiscatioun wes solemplie done, quhy insert ȝé nocht
þe instrument þairof, and consent of þe Scottis
Thre Estatis, and all judiciale process and con-
15 fiscatioun, or at þe lest quhy will ȝe nocht
allege sum historiciane for pruife, for þis surrenderence and confiscatioun ar greitar actis than
homageis.

Inglis.

Did nocht Kyng Henrie þe Fyift command ȝour kyng
20 of Scottis to attend on him in þe jornay for his
richt of France recouering?

Scott.

Nebour, ȝe play ȝour vaignes. ȝe handill þis as
ȝe do Scriptour. Quhilk kyng of Scottis maid þis

---

3 ȝour superiorite repeated MS.

attendance, quhat historiciane writis þe samyn?
I say, nocht ȝour Polidor.

f. 370^r Bot nebour, said ȝe nocht laitlie þat ȝour Kyng
Edward þe Thrid maid him-self be crownit Kyng of
5 Scotland and enioyit þe propreitie of þe samyn?
How hes Edward and ȝour kyngis departit so haista-
lie fra þe propreitie of Scotland, that commandis
within few ȝeiris nixt Scottis kyng to attend on
þair jornay in France? Be sic commandis apperis
10 þat nother þe surrenderence of Balliollis richt nor
þe semblance of confiscatioun was nouther just nor
of valeur aneuch.

Nichtbour, I traist ȝour kyngis movit of just con-
science as thai deposit þame-selffis and all þair
15 posterite fra þe propreitie of Scotland; sa be con-
science thai will frelie leif and ceiss to chal-
lange þat pretendit superiorite. Also, I will say
þat passage of ȝour Kyng Henry þe Fyft in France
wes about þe j^m iiij^c xv. ȝeir of Christ, and þe
20 Scottis crown come to þe Stewardis þe j^m iij^c lxx.
⎣ȝeir⎦ of Christ, and Robert þe Secund and Robert
þe Thrid, baith Stewardis, wes kyngis of Scotland
þe space l. ȝeiris or James Steward þe First was
Scottis kyng, quhais coronatioun wes maid fyve
25 ȝeiris eftir ȝour Kyng Henry the ⎣Fyftis⎦ passing
to France.

---

1 attendance added in margin MS.
21 ȝeir om. MS.
25 Fyftis MS. firstis

1 Cf. <u>Declaration</u>, sig. c iv^r (p. 202):

   And in this tyme the realme of Scotlande being
   descended to the house of the Stewardes, of which
   our Nephieu directly cometh, James Stuarde kynge
   of Scottis, in the yere of our lorde MCCCCXXIII.
   made homage to Henry the VI. at Wyndsour .....

8 Cf. <u>Angl. Hist</u>., p. 433:

   Sub Henrici mortem, Iacobus Steuartus Roberti regis
   Scoti unicus filius, nam Dauid maior natu alter
   filius iam antea perierat, ab Anglica classe capi-
   tur. Is duodecim natus annos, a patre in Galliam
   missus, ut apud principes Francos, mores & linguam
   addisceret, forte in naues Anglicas dum eo pro-
   ficisceretur incidit.

13 The Archduke Philip and his wife Joanna, queen of
   Castile were forced to seek refuge from storms while
   sailing from Zeeland to Spain in January 1506. They
   remained in England from 16 January to 23 April, during
   which period a number of agreements were reached, including one to the effect that Edmund de la Pole, duke
   of Suffolk, who had been a refugee at the court of
   Philip's father Maximilian since 1501, would be handed
   over to Henry VII. He was duly surrendered at Calais
   on 16 March, and taken to the Tower of London, where he
   remained until his execution on the orders of Henry
   VIII in 1513; on these diplomatic exchanges, see S.B.
   Chrimes, <u>Henry VII</u> (London 1972), pp. 92-4, 289-91.

Inglis.

ʒow, Scott, be ane vtwart man! Did noᴄht ʒour
Kyng James Steward þe First homage to Henrie þe vj.
in þe jᵐ iiijᶜ xxiij. ʒeiris?

Scott.

Nichtbour, quheir be all þe homagis þat þe Scottis
5   kyngis maid sen the jᵐ iijᶜ xlvj. ʒeiris? Sen ʒe
past oure þai homagis, I will noᴄht cumber my-
selff with þe impugnatioun of þame; bot to þis last
pretendit homage, ʒour Polidor writis thus: that
Kyng Robert Stewart of Scotland eftir þe deceiss of
10 his sone Dauid send James, his vthir sone, to
France, quha be tempest of sey wes drevin for
sauftie of lyfe in Ingland, tane and presentit to
ʒour kyng, as Philope, kyng of Castolie was to ʒour
Kyng Henrie þe vij., quha compellit þe samyn
15 Philope for to delyure guid Edmunde de la Pooll,
than fugitiue in Flanderis as in sanctuarie for
sauite of his life. Quhat þis James did or maid
in tyme of his captiuitie Scotland knawis noᴄht,
for he remanit þair xviij. ʒeiris or he wes kyng;
20 nor eftir his returnyng in Scotland þair wes
nouthir propreitie nor superiorite demandit at him
nor at þe Thre Estatis of Scotland.

f. 370ᵛ   Guid Man of Syon

We approche to þe town of Rowane. I counsell ʒow
continew this talking vnto þat we depart from þe

4   Cf. <u>Declaration</u>, sig. c iv^r (p. 202):

   All whiche homages and fealties as they appere by
   story to haue ben made and done at times and season
   as afore: so do there remayne instrumentes made
   thervpon and sealed with the seales of the kynges
   of Scotlande testifyenge the same.

towne, for now is tyme to speir eftir guid lugeing.

Inglis Merchand

Did I nocht luge ʒow weill and with ane mirrie
hostage? Bot guid maistiris, gife ʒe pleiss I will
returne to my purpoiss. Sayis nocht þe buik vpone
5   þe weris declaratioun þat all þir forsaid homagis
and fealteis, as þai appeir be historie to haif
bene maid and done at tym and seasoun as of afor,
so do thai remane instrumentis maid þairupone and
selit with þe selis of þe Scottis kyngis, teste-
10   feing þe sam be instrumentis vpone þair homagis and
fealteis etc.?

Scott.

ʒe haue left mekill labour to the redar for to
serche þe historijs for preving of all ʒour
homagis! Heirfor, gife ʒe preif þe forsaid pre-
15   tendit homagis na bettir be instrumentis and selis
nor ʒe haue done be historijs, I dreid þe redar
sall juge all ʒour homagis skant worth þe reding,
for neuer haue /ʒow/ allegit ane historiciane bot
Mariane alane, quhilk ʒe say wrett þe historie of
20   þe ix^c ʒeir of Christ; the quhilk Mariane, gif he
be ʒitt on lyfe and hes writtin þe homagis sen þat
tyme I can nocht say, bot he hes sufficient pruif
for aige!

---

18 ʒow om. MS.

Inglis.

Giff I will say þe craw is blak, than ʒow will say
þat scho is quhytt! Quhat man, dois it nocht
appeir be historie how ʒe Scottis practizate to
steill out of oure thesaurie diuerss of choiss
5   instrumentis, quhilk neuer-þe-les wes eftir recouerit agane?

Scott.

Nebour, so may I say: dois it nocht appeir be historie þat þe Inglismen buildit Rome? I pray ʒow,
nebour, quhat historiciane writtis þat þe Scottis
10   stall ʒour instrumentis?   For gife þis maner of
saying be admittit, ʒe may preif be historie quhat
ʒe list!

Nebour, sen ʒe grant and confessis þat ʒour stollin
euidentis war recouerit agane fra þe Scottis, it
15   semis honest þat ʒe serche and produce the recouerit instrumentis vpone þe pretendit homagis
for þe bettir probatioun of kyngis namis, placis
and tyme, þat ʒour buik of weir may be correctit
and amendit þairby etc.

f. 371^r   Inglis.

20   To þe intent þat thir thre honest men and ʒe may
knaw of quhat forme and tennour þe said instru-

_____

7   so may I say   corrected in MS. from ʒe may also
say

11 This is the translation of John Balliol's homage of
    December 1292 which is given in the <u>Declaration</u>, sig.
    c iv^v- d i^r.

mentis be, heir is insertit þe effect in word and
sentence as þai be maid, quhilk I do meit with þe
cavillatioun and contrewit evasioun of ʒow Scottis,
allegeing tha homagis to haif bene maid for þe
5   Erledome of Huntingtowne: tharfor þe tennour of þe
said instrument is thus . . . . .

Scott.

Nichtbour, now apperis ʒe go to þe secund maner of
probatioun, as be instrumentis, quharbe I beleif ʒe
sall do away all þe forsaid contradictioun of
10   kyngis ńames, placis and ʒeiris.

Inglis.

'I, Jhone N, kyng of Scottis, salbe trew and
faithfull vnto ʒow, lord Edward, be þe grace
of God kyng of Ingland, þe nobill and superior
lord of þe kyngdome of Scotland, and vnto ʒow
15   I mak my fedelite of þe sam kyngdome of Scotland, the quhilk I hald and clames to hald of
ʒow; and I sall beir to ʒow my faith and
fidelite of life and lym and wardlie honour
aganis all men; and faithfullie I sall knaw-
20   lege and sall do to ʒow seruice dew of þe
kyngdome of Scotland afoir said, as God so
help me and þir halie Evangelis.'

Scott.

Neboure, will ʒow inserte ony ma instrumentis?

_____
14 Scotland corrected in MS. from Ingland

Inglis.

Nay, faith, for þis ane is anew and sufficient!

Scott.

Nichtbour, I se ȝe haif endit ȝour pruif be ȝour
maner of historijs and gois to ȝour pruif of þis
pretendit homage be instrumentis. Nebour, gife
5   ȝe recouerit ȝour instrumentis fra þe Scottis
theifis as ȝe say ȝe did, ȝe suld haue insertit
ma instrumentis, or at þe leist þe forme and tennour of ane mair sufficient instrument for þe
bettir pruif of ȝour mater. Also, albeit thus
10 ȝour forsaid instrumentis war trew and formale,
ȝitt þe maner of þe inserting þairof is mair conforme to Kyng Williame þe Conqueroris lawis þan to
þe lovable custome in all vthir countreis, or to
þe Ciuile Law.

f. 371ᵛ
15 For, nichtbour, gife ony juge or redare suld decide this questioun, he mone do it outhir be þe
probatioun of þis ȝour preuate, perticulare in-
sertioun of instrument or ellis be þe extractioun
of þe sam instrument, justlie and trewlie ex-
20 tractit and authorisate be ane neutrale or twa
chosin men for to haue sene þe substance of þe
originale instrument, and also Scottis as partie
callit to þe sam effect; bot sic dew extractioun
is nocht obseruit. Heirfor as ȝe begouth þis
25 process of homage, sa consequenter ȝe follow
þairin. Now ȝe, guid man of Syon, of quhat

9   For Lamb's use of Polydore Vergil's discussion of
    these events, see above, 115/1-25.

18   See above, 95/1.

strynth or vigour hald ʒe ane instrument of homage
without þe name of him that makis þis homage, nocht
specifeand quhithir to þe first or last Edward,
kyng of Ingland, also without place, without ʒeir,

5   and witnes or notaris nam? And gife þe forsaid
instrument be þe witnessing of Jhone Balliolis
homage, as in deid apperis, than ʒour kyngis and
natioun of Ingland can attene small or litill
honour, as may be considerit in ʒour awin Poli-

10   dorus xvij. buik, and also insertit heir abufe.
Als, ʒow can nocht deny bot ʒour Kyng Henrie þe
Secund and Kyng Richard did homage to þe Kyng of
France for Normondie, Gasgony and Gyane; so did þe
Scottis for Northumberland and Huntingtown, for

15   Dauid, Kyng Alexanderis brothir, marijt Mathild,
dochtir and heretrice of Waldois, erle of Huntingtoun and Northumberland, quhilk Dauid becom Scottis
kyng eftir Alexander his brothiris deceiss. This
sayis and affirmis Polidor in his xiij. buik of

20   Inglis histore. Nebour, sen ʒe will þat ʒour
awin saying allone be sufficient pruif as of historie, I pray ʒow mak þe pruif of þir homagis be
instrumentis mair cleir.

                    Inglis.

I go to þe thrid maner of þir homagis pruif, be
25   recordis and registreis, quhilk we haue so formale,
so autenticale, so seriouslie handillit, and witht

---

3   quhithir added in margin MS.

7   This list occurs, in the same order, in the <u>Declar-</u>
    <u>ation</u>, sig. d i^r.

sic circumstancis declaring þe materis as thai be
and aucht to be a grit corroboratioun of þat hes
bene in historijs and reportit in þis mater; for
amangis vthir thingis we haue þe solempnit act and
5   judiciale process of Kyng Edwardis þe First in
dicisioun of þe titill of Scotland quhen þe sam
wes callangit be tuelff personis, that is to say,
be Florentinus comes Holandie, Patricius Dumbar
comes Marchie, Willelmus Vesty, Willelmus Roiss,
10   Robertus Pinbany, Nicholaus Sociles, Patricius
Galichtlie, Rogerus Mondevill, Johannes Cuming,
Johannes Haistingis, Johannes Balioll, Robertus
Bruiss, Ericus rex Noruegie; and finalie eftir
greit consultatioun, þe sentence wes gevin for þe
15   Baliole. Bot for þe confirmatioun of þe dewitie
of homage befor þat tyme obseruit be þe Scottis
kyngis, as it apperis in choiss recordis .....

f. 372^r   Scott.

I abide vnto ȝe insert þe forme and tennour of
ȝour recordis and registreis for þe thrid maner of
20   ȝour pruif of þir pretendit homagis befor Jhone
Balioll obseruit.

                     Inglis.

Quhat man, be ȝow deif or blind? Did nocht I
laitlie reherss þe registreis at full, and be þai
nocht in our thesaurie? Quhat can ȝow say bot þis

---

13 Ericus added in darker ink MS.
24 thesaurie   saurie added in darker ink MS.

record and registre be sufficient pruif?

Scott.

Nichtbour, than ȝe will þat þis ȝour report of
namis compeditouris of þe Scottis crown be as
sufficient pruif of so formale, so autenticall, so
5 seriouslie handillit and registrat with sic circumstancis! Neboure, did ȝour Conquerour institute
sic maner of proceding in judiciale actionis, sic
registring making in pleable materis? It apperis
weill þat þe registreis ar conforme to ȝour Con-
10 querouris lawis, and also to þe sentence þat Kyng
Edward gaife vpone þe discussioun of þe Scottis
crownis.

Sen ȝe haue as ȝour buik and also as ȝour-selff
sayis, this solempnit act and þis judiciale process
15 vpone þe discussioun of þe forsaid compeditouris
titill to þe realme of Scotland, ȝe can nocht
eschaip blame þat insert nocht in ȝour buik þe
forme and tennour of þe forsaidis compeditouris
compromit, the consent of Scotland þairto, also
20 Kyng Edwardis acceptatioun with examination of þe
caiss, the conclusioun and sentence; bot in sted of
all þe forsaid substantiall poyntis of weill ordanit registreis, ȝe and ȝour buik dois onlie expreme the compeditouris names and so mekill of þe
25 allegit sentence as makis for ȝow.

Neboure, quhat can þis guid man of Sion or ony
just man juge bot þis ȝour pruif be registreis, be

13   Cf. <u>Angl. Hist.</u>, pp. 323-4 (see above, 115/5-15).

---

16   veniretur   <u>MS</u>. veneretur
18   speciatim   <u>MS</u>. speciatum
20   domino   <u>MS</u>. dominio
25   arbitrum   <u>MS</u>. arbitrium
26   dominum   <u>MS</u>. dominium

recordis be also sufficient as ȝour pruif of historijs and instrumentis?

Neboure, it apperis ȝe haue nocht recouerit fra þe
Scottis ȝour allegit stollin instrumentis and
5   registreis, for and ȝe insert heir the tennour of
þame, peraduentour ȝe wald attene litill gáine and
less honour. Peraduentour ȝe think ȝour forsaid
record sufficientlie ordanit for to perswade ȝour
effect to þe Lundoun ladyis and to þe facill
10   Inglis peopill?

f. 372ᵛ Nebour, sen ȝe will nocht, I will report ane trew
register of þis mater, the quhilk ȝe can nocht
deny. Polidor in his xvij. buik writtis thus:
Scoti mortuo suo rege Alexandro, valde anxij quem
15   sibi regem optarent, et timentes ne dum de re
tanta inter se consultarent, ad vim /veniretur/,
ad Edwardum primum regem Anglorum legatos miserunt,
is respondit se velle /speciatim/ a Scotis principibus conceptis verbis jusiurandum sibi dari, vt
20   Scotie terre /domino/ atque cunctas regni arces
in suam potestatem tradi, ac cum demum se daturum
operam regi creando. Legati responso accepto,
mandata Edwardi ad principes Scotos sedulo detulerunt, quibus et si petitio visa est non solum as-
25   pera, verum etiam parum iusta vt Anglus non /ar-
bitrum/ regis creandi, sed /dominum/ Scotie ageret
attamen, quia inter se iam dissidebant, morem regi
gesserunt.

6 Cf. <u>Angl. Hist</u>., p. 324:

> Ioannes per hunc modum rex factus, primum omnium in
> uerba Edouardum iurat: dein in Scotiam reuersus ...
> magno cum totius populi gaudio coronatur.

14 Cf. <u>Angl. Hist</u>., p. 324:

> Is ut plus fauoris sibi conciliaret ab Anglis, eg-
> regias Oxonij ædificauit ædes, eoque loci collegi-
> um scholasticorum instituit, & illud possessionibus
> locupletauit, ac ab se, Baliolense collegium nomi-
> nauit.

Heirfore ʒe haue hard þe competitouris compromit,
Scotlandis consent þarto, the maner of Kyng Edwardis acceptatioun of þe compromit, þe exam-
inatioun of þe mater; now pleis ʒow heir þe con-
5   clusioun, and also þe just sentence. Polidor
writtis þir wordis: <u>Johannes Baliolus per hunc</u>
<u>modum rex factus, primum omnium in verba Edwardi</u>
<u>iurat, deinde in Scotiam reuersus magno cum totius</u>
<u>populi gaudio coronatur.</u> Ʒe haue hard now þe just
10 sentence, þe forme, and also afoir laitlie þe
tenno<u>u</u>r of þe forsaid instrument.

'I, Jhone N., kyng of Scottis, salbe trew and
faithfull vnto ʒow, lord Edward, be þe grace of
God kyng of Ingland etc.' Als Polidor writis
15 forder: <u>Is Johannes Baliolus vt plus fauoris sibi</u>
<u>conciliaret ab Anglis, egregias Oxonie edificauit</u>
<u>edes, eoque loci collegium scolasticorum instituit,</u>
<u>et illud possessionibus locupletauit, ac ab se</u>
<u>Baliolense Collegium nominauit.</u>

20 Nebour, knaw ʒe quhat ane aith is <u>jusiurandum</u>
<u>conceptis verbis</u>? This be no<u>ch</u>t þe comown forme
of homage-making, bot ane tiranfull charge.

Nebour, do ʒe no<u>ch</u>t knaw quhatt þir wordis menis:
<u>atque ciuitas regni arces in suam potestatem</u>
25 <u>tradi</u>? Or evir Kyng Edward wald accept the compromit, this be ʒour kyngis sentence; syn follow-

---

1   compromit <u>corrected in MS. from</u> comptent
5   just <u>added in margin MS.</u>
15 sibi <u>added in margin MS.</u>

is *primum omnium verba Edwardi jurat*, the quhilk
is þe forsaid instrumentis homage.

'I, Jhone N., kyng of Scottis ...' Also Polidor
sayis ferder: *deinde in Scotiam reuersus ... coro-*
5   *natur*. Be þir wordis it apperis weill þat þis
aitht wes maid in Ingland, or Jhone Baliole past
in Scotland to be coronate.

f. 373^r Now, guid man of Sion, I traist 3e think þat part
of greit princis deidis is mair to be merwalat
10   than to be followit?

Inglis.

Giffe 3e Scottis will tak exceptioun to þe homagis
of 3our princis as maid in weir and by force,
quhilk is nocht trew, quhat can 3ow say aganis
3our awin Perliament, testefeit be 3our awin selis
15   and writtingis?

Scott.

Nebour, we ken na weir þat causis our kyngis mak
sic homage. Nebour, gife 3e mynd of Brutus
parliament, quharin he devidit þe haill ile of
Britane amangis his thre sonnis and gaif þe souer-
20   antie of his twa sonnis to Lotus, his eldest sone,
gife þis be þe parliament þat 3e mynd, the Scottis
will misknaw bayth þe selis and hand-writt, and

---

3   N. interlin. MS.
21 þe interlin. MS.;   MS. also has þe interlin.
    after parliament

2 See above, 143/13.

15 This seems to be a piece of misrepresentation on
Lamb's part, for the Declaration makes no such statement.

---

4 veniretur MS. veneretur
6 speciatim MS. speciatum
8 domino MS. dominio
25 to om. MS.
27 Henrie þe viij. cancelled MS.

gife ȝe mynd as ȝour Polidor writis in his xvij.
buik: <u>Scoti mortuo rege suo Alexandro, valde</u>
<u>anxii quem sibi regem optarent, et timentes ne dum</u>
<u>de re tanta inter se consultarent, ad vim /veni-</u>
5   <u>retur/, ad Edwardum primum legatos miserunt, is</u>
<u>respondit se velle /speciatim/ a Scotis principibus</u>
<u>conceptis verbis jusiurandum sibi dari, vt Scotie</u>
<u>terre /domino/ atque cunctas regni arces in suam</u>
<u>potestatem tradi, et cum demum se daturum operam</u>
10   <u>regi creando.</u> Giffe þis Polidorus writing be trew,
ȝe may considdir quhar, quhy and quhen þis aith
wes gevin, for it wes maid befor or þe Baliolis
richt wes decidit, and also or he wes crownit, and
no<u>ch</u>t eftir Baliolis coronatioun as ȝour Kyng
15   Henrie þe viij. menit in his Declaratioun of Weir.
Now þe Scottis ar content for to gife to þe Inglis
kyngis all þe hono<u>u</u>r þat þai may justlie attene be
þis Scottis Perliament consent allegit be ȝow.

Inglis.

Thus apperis vnto ȝow þe begy<u>n</u>ing of þis superi-
20   orite, with a perpetuale co<u>n</u>tinewance, without
intermissioun within memorie? Bot a certan
omissioun and forbering vpone groundis and occasionis forsaid; we deny no<u>ch</u>t bot as ȝour kyngis
detractit þe doing of þair dewitie, so God grantit
25   vnto ws, þe realme of Ingland, force for /to/
compell ȝow þar̲to within memorie, except fra þe
tym of Kyng Henrie þe vi. to þe xxxiij. ȝeir of

Kyng Henrie þe viij., in þe quhilk tyme how þe
realme of Ingland had bene lacerate and vexit it
is ane lamentable thing for to be rehersit.

f. 373^{V} Also Kyng Henrie þe viii. culd no<u>ch</u>t persew this
5   richt of homage be minorite of his nephew, being
       þan mair cairfull how to bring him out of danger
       to þe place of a kyng þan to resaue of him homage;
       quharfor being senshence þe last homage maid be þe
       Scottis kyngis to Kyng Henrie þe vj. in þe j^{m}
10   iiij^{c} xxiij. ȝeiris of Christ is comptit j^{c} xxii.
       ȝeiris to þis instant ȝeir j^{m} v^{c} xlij. ȝeiris of
       Christ, of þe quhilk j^{c} xxij. ȝeiris þair wes lvj.
       ȝeiris in contentioun for þe crown of Ingland,
       quharof truble ingenderit and also sum busynes,
15   xxiiij. ȝeiris in þe tym of Kyng Henrie þe vij.,
       and also in Kyng Henrie þe viij. tym xxj. ȝeiris
       of forbering for to dema<u>n</u>d þe said superiorite in
       tyme of Kyng James þe Fyftis minorite, and so
       finalie þe Scottis resorting to ȝo<u>ur</u> onlie defence
20   of discontinuence of possessioun can onlie allege
       justlie bot xiij. ȝeiris of sylence in our Kyng
       Henrie þe viij. tyme, quhilk xiij. ȝeiris ar past
       our sen þe outpassing of ȝo<u>ur</u> Kyng James þe Fiftis
       minorite. Law nor reasoun seruis no<u>ch</u>t þat þe
25   passing oure of a tym no<u>ch</u>t co<u>mm</u>odius for þe pur-
       poiss for to be allegeable in prescriptioun for
       loss of ony richt; quhilk impedime<u>n</u>t being last
       on ȝow Scottis pairt, þe haill prescriptioun, gife

---

12 lvj. <u>corrected in MS. from</u> xxij.

27   As it occurs in the MS., this reference is scarcely
     intelligible. It seems, however, that Lamb intends an

þe mater war prescriptable, is thus deducit eui-
dentlie to xiij. ȝeiris, in þe quhilk tym Kyng
Henrie þe viij. hes ceissit and forborne to demand
his dewitey. Bot no<u>ch</u>t for þat causs dois he entir
5   þis <u>present</u> weir, nor myndit to demand ony sic
mater, all-tho<u>ch</u>t sic be þe werkis of God, superi-
o<u>ur</u> our all, to suffir occasionis be ministrat
quharby dew superiorite may be demandit.

Scott.

Nichtbour, I speir at ȝow gife þis be ȝour maner of
10   proceding in pleable materis, na juge being ordi-
nar<u>ie</u> nor be parteis chosin, the defendar ne<u>uer</u>
being su<u>mm</u>ond, that þe actor allone sall propone
þe questioun, alane sall accept reply and wse
domesticall pruif, sall concluid, and also þat
15   selff actor sall pronu<u>n</u>ce þe sentence diffinitiue?
This proceding vsis ȝo<u>ur</u> kyngis buik on þe declaratioun of þis instant weir. Nebour, ȝe haue maid
ane epilog and schort reherss of þis <u>p</u>re<u>te</u>ndit
homage, quhilk be na labour nor way can bring fur<u>th</u>
20   of dirknes to licht, for þis superioritie wantis na
thing bot guid ground <u>and</u> veritie, and also
sufficient probatioun.

The diuisionis of Brittane and þe homagis maid in
Brutus tyme ȝe mak mair apparent than ony homagis
25   sen-syn, for þe nerther ȝe bring the homagis to j^m
v^c xlij. ȝeiris of Christ ȝour pruif ry<u>n</u>nis the
fastar abak fra ȝow, as dois þe ⌊stone⌋ from Siphus.
_____
27   stone <u>MS</u>. sone

allusion to the legend of Sisyphus, who was condemned
to push a large stone to the top of a hill in Hell,
only to see it roll to the bottom again. This endless
cycle was a punishment for his dishonesty. Cf. Homer,
Odyssey, xi, 593-600; Ovid, Metamorphoses, iv, 460.

25   Alexander, lord Hume occurs as Chamberlain between 2
     October 1513 and 18 July 1514 (RMS., iii, nos. 2-22),
     but was among the anti-Albany faction and after twice
     fleeing to England was arrested in March 1516 and
     executed on 8 October. Lamb rightly stresses his
     power as a Border magnate, but he glosses over the
     political difficulties of the period.

Quhen suld þe pruif of þis homage bene cleir bot
in freschenes and neir memorie of man, þat is within þe last j^c xxij. ȝeir, at quhilk ȝeiris begyning
ȝe say our Kyng James þe First maid homage to Kyng
5   Henry þe vj.? ȝe pruif this homage be na historiciane nor instrument nor register, bot gife it be
Marian, ane Scottis writtar, quhombe ȝour buik
pruffis all þe homagis maid sen þe ix^c ȝeir of
Christ!

f. 374^r

10   I haue answerit befoir to þis pretendit homage of
Kyng James þe First; bot as I juge, nebour, þir
homagis of þir last j^c xxij. ȝeir I hald ȝe haue
provin best the vexatioun of Ingland and minorite
of Kyng James þe Fyft, becaus it is alyk to allege
15   historijs, instrumentis and registreis in generale
as to allege nane at all.

Nichtbour, now I will say to carfulnes of ȝour Kyng
Henrie the viii. for his nephew, kyng of Scotland,
bayth Ingland and Scotland knawis, and so will þe
20   posterite knaw, þe cairfulnes þat Kyng Henrie the
viij. bure, nocht onlie to his nephew bot also to
vthiris of his awin bluid, to his tendir familiaris, and also to þe nobilite of Ingland.

Nebour, I will schaw to ȝow twa thingis quhilk maid
25   ȝour Kyng Henrie þe viij. cairfull: first, þat his
nephew had þat tyme Lord Hume Greit Chalmerland and
Generale Wardan, quhilk mycht within xviij. houris

---

27 xviij. corrected in MS. from xliij.

3 John, duke of Albany, first cousin to James IV, was
   appointed governor in the aftermath of Flodden and
   arrived in Scotland in May 1515. He remained for two
   years, but was absent in France from 1517 to 1521 and
   again in 1522-3. He departed for the last time in May
   1524, and his governorship was formally ended on 16
   November. Power was, however, already in the hands of
   a faction sympathetic to England, led by the earl of
   Arran and Margaret Tudor.

10 This calculation is wrong (see above, 33/4); James V
    did not turn twelve until April 1524. But the sack of
    Jedburgh did in fact take place in the autumn of 1523,
    not in 1519.

convenit x^m horsmen for to haue done ane act a contra Ingland; the vthir thing wes þat þe Scottis
kyng, ʒour kyngis nephew, had Jhone, duik of Albany, þe maist expert and maist doutit capitane of
5   weir in his dayis, tutour and gouernour of Scotland. Sa lang as þe Chalmerland wes on life and
þis duik of Albany in authorite and credit, ʒour
kyng attemptit no weir contrar Scotland; bot how
sone þir two was departit fra authorite the vncle,
10 cairfull of þe nephew (being of xij. ʒeiris of
aige in þe j^m v^c xix. ʒeir), send Thomas, duik of
Norphok with ane army in Scotland to wast Teviothdaill, birn þe town and abbay of Jedburth, kest
doun castellis and haldis. The deid þairof ʒitt
15 remanis to pruif.

Do ʒe nocht remember þat eftir þat birnyng followit in þe j^m v^c xxxij. ʒeiris of Christ twa tendir
and familiar meting in Ardriss, Calico and Bullone
of ʒour Kyng Henrie þe viij. with Franciss, kyng
20 of France, and how eftir þat metingis in þe j^m v^c
xxxij. ʒeiris of Christ þe sam Kyng Henrie maid
weir vpone his nephew of Scotland?

Do ʒe nocht als remember Kyng Henrie þe vncle mantenit all his lifetym certan Scottis nobillis,
25 abyding on a vait for to noy and weir one his
nepheu of Scotland, and syn persavand no prosperite of his weir contractit pece for to indure
for þe langar leuear of þe vncle and nephew? This
is provin be þe contract of pece and seill of
30 Ingland.

2 On Bowes and the battle at Haddon Rig, see above,
   51/19. The date is there given as 22 August, which is
   more probably correct; but St Bartholomew's Day is 24
   August.

16 David II was born on 5 March 1324, and was four years
    old when he was married to Joan of England as part of
    the peace settlement of 1328 (see below, 163/25). The
    Balliol faction, acting with English support, returned
    to Scotland in August 1332; Edward III recaptured Ber-
    wick in July of the following year, and David II's
    position had deteriorated sufficiently by the spring
    of 1334 for him to take refuge in France. He did not
    return until 1341.

Do ȝe nocht remember how Kyng Henrie þe vncle send
Schir Robert Bowis and v^m men a contra his nepheu,
and wes tane at Halding Rig witht all his cumpany
on Sanct Bartholomeus Day in þe j^m v^c xlij. ȝeir?
5   This neidis na vthir pruif þan þe deid selff.

f. 374^v Do /ȝe/ nocht remember how þe said duik of Norphok
wes send a contra the nephew witht a greit army of
xl^m men and nobilite of Ingland, and also ȝour
greit navy of schippis, in þe said j^m v^c xlij.
10   ȝeiris of Christ?

This Kyng Henry onlie schew semblable cairfulnes
for his nephew that Kyng Edward þe First schew in
þe deciding of þe richt vpone þe crown of Scotland,
and as Edward þe Thrid schew to Dauid, kyng of
15   Scotland, his guid-brothir, haifand Johanna, Kyng
Edwardis þe Secundis dochtir, to wyff, and beand
bot ten ȝeiris of aige; this Edward þe Thrid
ceissit nocht quhill he chaist sistir and guid-
brothir bayth out of Scotland to France.

20   Bot it apperis cleirlie þat all þir forsaid carfulnes wes done becaus þe vncle had vodit Ingland
of nobillis, of wyss men and familiaris, and of
his agnetis, and couth nocht be na vthir craftie
wayis bring his nephew fra obedience of God, fra
25   þe alliance of France to be ane defendar of his
new factioun of Ingland, sikand vnder þe pretence
of a disapoyntit meting at ȝork and vthir four

---

6 ȝe om. MS.
26 sikand corrected in MS. from sic

16   Lamb must here be referring to the letter of quit-
     claim by which Edward III of England (and not Edward
     II, as he mistakenly believes) acknowledged Robert I
     as king of Scotland and renounced the English claim to
     superiority. This letter, written at York on 1 March
     1328, must have been in the Scottish archives in 1549,
     but the original is now lost; the text is given, from
     a notarial copy which has also disappeared but which
     was printed by Thomas Innes in the eighteenth century,
     in Stones, Anglo-Scottish Relations, pp. 322-5. Lamb
     gives an accurate summary of the main points, but the
     agreement to a marriage between Edward III's sister
     Joan and David Bruce actually occurs in a second docu-
     ment, an indenture completed at Edinburgh on 17 March
     1328, which does survive and which is printed, ibid.,
     pp. 328-41. It is clear that Lamb must have been
     working from the documents themselves.

vane, truffill causis afoir specifeit and sufficientlie impugnit, witht a superioritie allegit and
socht with greit labour and calculat a gemino ouo,
as sa had bene in veritie.

5   And gife ȝour buik culd haue fund and imaginit mair
causis or trewar, I doubt nocht bot þe samyn had
bene done for bettir justificatioun of þis weir.
For probatioun of þis my present allegeance, I
refer to þe nobilitie, of commonis of bayth Ingland
10   and Scotland.

Also, we Scottis reputis ws to haue bettir titill
and defence þan prescriptioun, þe quhilk we need
nocht moir to proif þan þe Inglis courtisianis
nedis to pruif ȝour selffis maid nothir of stok nor
15   stane.

Forder, nebour, þe Scottis hes ane evident vnder
þe Greit Seill of Ingland, quharin ȝour Kyng Edward þe Secund, with þe consent of þe nobilite and
Thre Estatis of Ingland, confessis þai neuer had
20   sic a pretendit superiorite of Scotland, and gife
ony wes maid be Jhone Balioll or ony vthir of
Scotland þai renuncit þe samyn and pronuncit for
þame-selffis and þair posterite of Ingland to Kyng
Robert þe Bruse neuer to callenge his superioritie
25   in tym cuming, and for confirmatioun of þe samyn
Kyng Edward þe Thrid delyuerit Johanna, his sistir,
to be marijt on Dauid, Kyng Robertis sone.

Forder, gife sic superioritie had bene, we repute

ane greit honour for to haue fred our-selffis fra
sic thirlage.

Nebour, may veritie satefie ʒow Inglismen, this
forsaid euident is mater in deid, and no<u>ch</u>t
5   stollin furt<u>h</u> of þe Scottis Thesaurie!

f. 375^r   Nebour, as God hes gevin vnto þe Inglismen force
to mak ws Scottis knaw our sy<u>n</u>nis, so þe samy<u>n</u> God
hes gevin vnto Scottis force to mak þe court of
Ingland to knaw þair hethand pryd.

10   Nebour, ʒe say sic: I find nouthir in ʒour buik nor
be ʒo<u>u</u>r-selff þat j^c xxij. ʒeiris afoir ne<u>m</u>mit wes
ony requisitioun of homage maid be ʒo<u>u</u>r kyngis,
nor also in na kyngis tyme of befoir.

Now, guid man of Sion, I beleif ʒe haue reid þe
15   buik vpoun þe declaratioun of þis <u>present</u> weir,
and als ʒe haue hard how sufficientlie þe Ingliss
merchand hes repetit þe samy<u>n</u>, hes provin all þis
<u>prete</u>ndit homagis fra þe ix^c ʒeir of Christ to þe
j^m v^c xlij. ʒeir be historijs of Scottis Marian
20   allane, the quhilk Marianis buikis <u>and</u> writtingis
ar na mair knawin in Scotland than Tuball Cain
werkis, and sine how puirlie he hes provin ane
instrume<u>n</u>t allane, quharin is no<u>ch</u>t co<u>n</u>tenit the
homage-makeris name, nor þe name to quhome it wes
25   maid, nor place, day, ʒeir, witnes, nor notaris
name; also, last of all, ʒe haue hard how waiklie
he hes provin be registreis.

---

6 as <u>interlin. MS.</u>

In lyk wyss, guid man of Syon, ȝe haue hard our
ansuer to þe disapoyntit meting, our evacuatioun
of þe spuilȝeis allegit committit be þe Scottis;
also ȝe haue hard our refewing of þe detenit
5   Inglis rebellis, and our pretence for þe pretendit
vsurpatioun of þe bitt of barrat muir.

In lyk wyiss, guid man of Syon, ȝe haif hard my
impugnatioun of þir pretendit homagis, provin be
Polidor and be contradictioun of þe buik selff on
10   þir weris declaratioun, quhilk þe ilk Polidor
aggreis nouthir on kyngis namis, ȝeir, day nor
place.

Guid man of Syon, I say ane thing for to concluid:
þe weltht and insolence of Inglis court, and to it
15   þe excessius obedience of Inglis nobilitie, enterit þis present weir, and all vthir tymes makis
semblable besynes our all; bot sen ȝe haue hard
and red þe continew of þe buik vpone þe declaratioun of þis weir, and also hard þe impugnatioun
20   of þe sam buik, now restis onlie in ȝour hand þe
justificatioun of þis weir.

Guid man of Syon

Guid freindis, I haue red Kyng Henrie þe viij.
buik vpone the declaratioun of þis present weir,
quharin I persaue nocht a formale judiciall pro-
25   cess vpon ȝour questioun, becaus þis buik makis

---

1   lyk   interlin. MS.
17   besynes   added in margin MS.

ane self man persewar, defendar, juge, scrybe, witnes, and als gevar of sentence, quhilk is by /no͞/
sic consuetud þat I haue sene.   Bot, Scott, nou-
f. 375ᵛ thir pertenis to ȝow / nor to þis gentill-man of
5   Ingland for to refer þis gritt disputabill questioun to a finale determinatioun of ony man; also
it is mair wechtie than efferis for to decern
vpone.   Bot ȝow haif maid mony valid improbationis
quhilk /I͞/ and my cumpanionis, quhome ȝe and this
10   Inglisman hes chosin juge, can nor will decern
þaron vnto we haue red Polidor, quhom ȝe bring for
pruif of ȝour improbationis.   Bot, guid freind
Scott, ȝe did laitlie juge me effectionat to
Inglismen: I pray ȝow hald me na mair effectionat
15   to þame nor to þe veritie.   Quhen I did hant in
Ingland, þair regnit ane nobill prince, Kyng Henrie
þe viij., quhais naturale guidnes wes oftymes
alterat be counsell.   Also þan þe new leirnyng of
Germanie entiris in his court — quhat, be þis
20   kyng deith?

Inglis merchand

Ȝe, faitht, he is depairtit of þis wardill.

Guid man of Syon

I am sorie þairfoir, for than I think þe court
sall nocht onlie þe new leirnyng for to incresche

---

2 no   om. MS.
9 I   om. MS.

7 This doctrine is also cited by the author of The Complaynt of Scotland (ed. Stewart, p. 26):

> Socrates techit in his achademya, sayand, that eftir seuyn ande thretty thousand ʒeiris, al thingis, sal retourne, to that sammyn stait, as thai began, ande he to be borne agane in his mother voymbe, ande to be neurist til his aige, and sal teche philosophie in athenes. dionisius sal exsecute his ald tirranye in siracuse. Iulius cesar sal be lord of rome, ande annibal sal conques ytalie ...

Transmigration of souls is discussed in several of Plato's dialogues (e.g. Republic, x, 617-9; Timæus, 41-2; Phædo, 70-81), but the normal interval between incarnations is given as 10,000 years, rather than 37,000 or 48,000, in Phædrus, 249.

9 The doctrine of metempsychosis is attributed to Pythagoras by Aristotle, De anima, 407 b20; cf. Porphyry, Vita Pythagoræ, 19. There is a useful discussion of the question in J.A. Philip, Pythagoras and Early Pythagoreanism (Toronto 1966), pp. 151-6.

amangis þe nobillis and commonis of Ingland, bot
als able to renew þe auld philosophouris opinionis,
quhilkis makis me soir addred for to decerne in
þis 3our questioun.

5   For quha dois knaw gife I sall returne and traffict
in Ingland xlviij^m 3eir eftir þis as we traffictit
in þe j^m v^c xxxv. 3eir of Christ, as menit Plato?

Or quha knawis giffe my saull at departing gayis
in ane vthir mannis body, as menit Pethagoras, or
10   þat I be disburijt as sum was in Ingland eftir he
had lyue in erth thre hundreth 3eiris? For sic
chancis I hald na wisdome for to gife mater vnto
mun3eonis of Inglis court for to blame me befor
Kyng Henrie þe viij., þe quhilk will ringne in
15   Ingland agane eftir þis xlviij^m 3eir. Also, we
thre at þat tyme will traffict in Ingland, as þe
philosophoure menit, for þan most we induir agane
þe scharp persequutioun of court. Bot sen we man
repoiss in Pareiss, I will consult with þe leirnit
20   men quhat be þe trewth of Platois and Pithagoras
opinionis: þaireftir we sall commown ferder on þis
questioun, and also on þe vthir buik etc.

GLOSSARY

This Glossary is not intended to list all the words and forms found in the text, but as an aid to its reading. It does not include forms which are still standard, or, for the most part, words in near-standard spellings with meanings which are still current. In the case of the more common words, only the first three occurrences are generally noted.

A

abak, adv., *backwards*, 155/27.

abbay, n., *abbey*, 31/7, 159/13.

abill, adv., *perhaps*, 17/12, 25/18, 27/2 [var. of ablins; OF. able, L. habilis].

abillast, adj., *most fit*, 89/19.

abstinatlie, adv., *obstinately*, 111/19.

abufe, adv., *above*, 139/10.

abyde, v., *stop, stay*, 61/10; *abyding*, pres. p. *staying*, 159/25.

a contra, prep., *against*, 15/7, 17/15, 27/10 etc.

acceptatioun, n., *acceptance*, 115/16, 143/20.

accomptit, n., *accounted considered*, 81/2.

accustummat, p.p., *accustomed*, 47/20.

actioun, n., *legal proceedings*, 19/26.

actor, n., *pursuer* (leg.), 155/12.

addand, pres.p., *adding*, 11/6.

addred, adj., *fearful*, 171/3.

adiugit, pret., *determined* 119/23. [this sense not in DOST].

advysit, p.p., *considered*, 17/25; **weill advysit**, adj., *well-counselled*, 9/8.

adwyiss, n., *advice, opinion*, 15/2, 39/15.

affectionat, adj., *prejudiced, biased*, 13/10; **effectionat**, 9/19, 169/13, 169/14.

afor, conj., prep., *before*, 61/22, 131/7; **afoir**, 147/10, 165/11; **a-foir**, 27/17.

aganis, prep., *against*, 35/12, 39/1, 57/13 etc.

aggre, v., *be similar (to), be in conformity (with)*, 9/15; **aggreis**, *is in conformity with*, 103/17, 109/19, 167/11; **aggreit**, p.p. adj., 73/24.

aggreable, adj., *in conformity with*, 65/2.

aggrege, v., *exaggerate the seriousness of*, 37/2 [OF aggreger].

agit, adj., *aged*, 125/9.

agnet, n., *kinsman on the father's side*, 89/19; **agnetis**, 161/23.

aige, n., *age*, 31/9, 117/20, 121/8.

aikiris, n.pl., *acres*, 45/23, 47/18.

air, n., *heir*, 27/13, 27/16, 39/21, (?)57/8; **airis**, 35/9.

aith, n., *oath*, 147/20, 151/11; **aitht**, 149/6.

aither, adj., *other*, 121/28; **athir**, 25/2, 51/9.

alane, adj., *only*, 5/8, 19/9, 155/13; **allane**, 165/23.

alanerlie, adv., *only*, 17/2, 55/25, 81/14 etc.

albeit, conj., *although*, 45/13, 73/23, 137/9.

allargeit, pret., *enlarged*, 69/16.

allegationis, n. pl., *arguments*, 61/8; *assertions*, 157/14.

allege, v., *claim, assert*, 119/18; **allegeing**, pres. p., 135/4; **allegit**, pret., 65/16.

allegeable, adj., *capable or being asserted or claimed*, 153/26.

allegeance, n., *assertion, allegation*, 19/25, 85/21, 107/17 etc.

almaist, adv., *almost*, 37/18, 159/23.

als, adv., conj., *also*, 13/14, 17/10, 19/11 etc.; **als ... as**, *as ... as*, 91/2.

alsua, adv., *also*, 77/18; **alswa**, 109/4.

alterat, p.p., *changed*, 169/18.

alyk, adj., *the same*, 157/14.

amangis, prep., *amongst*, 31/12, 45/12, 141/4.

ambaxatouris, n.pl., *ambassadors*, 23/25, 27/2, 27/11, etc.

amite, n., friendship, 21/15, 29/4; ? *alliance*, 23/27, 31/2, 37/25 [OF. amite, amitie].

and, conj., **and**, 3/2 etc.; *if*, 3/3, 13/2.

ane, indef. art., 3/1 etc., numeral, *one*, 3/12, 5/11.

aneuch, adj., adv., *enough*, 127/12; **anew**, 137/1.

anis, adv., *once*, 101/1; **at anis**, *at once*, 57/15; **attonis**, 57/19.

apperand, pres.p., adj., *apparent*, 27/15, 27/29.

apperandlie, adv., *apparently*, 79/25, 117/15.

appeir, v., *appear*, 5/7, 49/27, 131/6 etc.; **apperis**, pres., 11/4, 19/17, 21/6; **apperit**, pret., 31/20.

appoynt, v., *arrange*, 33/3; **appoyntit**, p.p., adj., 31/19, 51/27.

appoynting, vbl. n., *arrangement*, 37/1.

appoyntmentis, n.pl., *arrangements*, 31/11.

appruife, v., *prove, demonstrate*, 17/4.

appunct, v., *arrange*, 35/15, 41/18; **appunctit**, pret., 31/2, 33/14; p.p. 7/7, 31/13 [Med.L. appunctuare].

arbitrale, adj., *by or of an arbiter;* **decrete arbitrale**, *legal judgment by an arbiter*, 119/24.

asselȝe, v., *attack*, 37/15 [OF. asaillir].

athir, *see* **aither**.

attendance, n., *personal presence*, 127/1 [This sense not in DOST but cf. ME]; **geif attendance**, *listen*, 13/18, 15/1.

attene, v., *obtain*, 25/16, 145/6, 151/17.

attonis, *see* **anis**.

attoure, adv., *moreover*, 91/2.

aucht, v., *ought*, 141/2.

aucht, num. adj., *eighth*, 5/15, 5/20, 7/8 etc.; **Auch**, 27/9.

auld, adj., *old*, 19/7.

auctor, n., *author*, 65/13.

autentick, adj., *authoritative, reliable*, 17/19, 17/24, 21/3 etc.; **autentik**, 57/6; **autenticall**, 143/4 [earliest example of this form in DOST 1576; e.mod.E. from *c.*1531].

autentikle, adv., *authentically, genuinely*, 9/6; **autenticle**, 15/14; **attentiklie**, 55/21.

autenticale, adv., *authentically, genuinely*, 139/26 [Not in DOST].

autentikenes, n., *authenticity*, 17/17, 19/22 [Earliest example in DOST Bisset, 1622–6].

authorisate, adj., p.p., *authorized*, 15/15, 17/9, 17/17 etc.; **authorisat**, 5/18.

authorisate, pret., *authorized*, 101/5 [Earliest in DOST Rolland, *c.*1550].

authorite, n., *authority*, 9/8 [Earliest in DOST Q Kennedy, 1558 but cf. ME].

avoding, vbl. n., *avoiding*, 59/3.

awin, adj., *own*, 5/3, 19/10, 19/19 etc.

awnare, n., *owner*, 123/15; **awnaris**, 27/2.

ay, adv., *always*; **ay as ȝitt**, *always until now*, 69/24.

B

baith, adj. and adv., *both*, 47/18; **bayth**, 17/18, 21/17, 25/17 etc.

band, n., *bond, agreement*, 125/10.

barrate, adj., *poor, valueless*, 45/23; **barrat**, 167/16.
battale, n., *battle*, 37/13; **battell**, 37/17.
be, prep., conj., *by*, 5/14, 31/18, 37/20 etc.
beand, pres.p., *being*, 23/22, 31/8, 31/10 etc.
befoir, conj., adv., prep., *before*, 33/23
begouth, pret., *began*, 15/18, 21/18, 63/5 etc.
behind, adv., *after*, 93/2.
behuvit, pret., *was necessary*, 39/19.
beild, v., *build*, 63/26, 83/6; **beildis**, pres., 71/17.
belief, v., *believe*, 29/19; **belevit**, pret., 33/21.
besynes, n., *purpose, occupation*, 3/4.
bett, pret., *beat*, 5/5.
betuene, prep., *between*, 21/16.
betuix, prep., *between*, 3/2, 13/17, 19/8 etc.
birne, v., *burn*, 31/6.
birning, vbl. n., *burning*, 31/17.
bluid, n., *blood*, 45/7; *breed*, 53/14.
bordour, n., *border, frontier*, 29/1, 47/23; **bordouris**, 23/9, 43/10.
bordouraris, n. pl., *borderers*, 23/14, 47/23.
borrow, v., *redeem, ransom*; **God to borrow**! (oath), 17/16.
bot, bott, prep., *except, other than*, 17/8, 17/18, 37/8 etc.; adv., *only*, 45/23, 55/25, 65/26 etc.; conj., *but*, 3/13, 5/8, 9/15 etc.; **bot gife**, *unless*, 93/6, 157/6.
bounding, pres.p. adj., *extending*, 69/26.
boundis, n. pl., *boundary, limits*, 7/17.
breiking, vbl. n., *breaking, violating*, 37/2.
brek, v., *break*, 7/7, 37/2; **brekis**, pres., 51/10; **brak**, pret., 33/18; **brokin**, p.p. adj., 53/17.
brethering, n. pl., *brothers*, 59/9.
brint, p.p. adj., *burned*, 31/18.
brocht, pret., *brought*, 23/11; p.p., 33/22.
buik, n., *book*, 5/11, 49/9, 49/22 etc.; **buikis**, 7/1, 9/7, 13/6 etc.
bure, pret., *bore*, 157/21.
byar, n., *buyer*, 125/2.

C

cairfull, adj., *taking care, concerned*, 153/6, 157/25, 159/10. [Earliest example in DOST of this sense 1568 but found in e. ME and later].

cairfulnes, n., *concern*, 157/20, 161/11; **carfulnes**, 157/17, 161/20.

calcalatioun, n., *calculation*, 73/24. [Earliest example in DOST 1570].

calculing, vbl. n., *calculation*, 97/4, 99/8, 107/10 etc. [Not in DOST, but *calcul*, v., attested from 1538].

callange, v., *accuse, challenge*, 37/21; **callenge**, 163/24; **callangit**, pret., 141/7.

castellis, n. pl., *castles*, 31/7, 31/17.

cavillation, n., *quibbling, contention*, 135/3.

ceissit, pret., *desisted*, 155/3.

chalmer, n., *chamber, room*; **Prevay Chalmer**, 35/24.

Chamerland, n., *Chamberlain*, 157/26, 159/6.

chesit, pret., *chased*, 71/3.

childring, n. pl., *children*, 5/5, 63/4, 113/5.

choiss, adj., *choice*, 141/17.

cietie, n., *city*, 101/17.

ciuiliteis, n. pl., *cultured habits*, 63/5. [Earliest example in DOST Arbuthnot but in e.m.E. from 1549].

clemence, n., *clemency*, 87/11.

comittar, n., *committer*, 23/6.

commit, p.p. adj., *come*, 35/3.

commodius, adj., *convenient*, 37/14, 37/20, 153/25.

commonyng, n., *discussion*, 13/13, 15/3, 55/2 etc.

comown, v., *talk, discourse*, 13/6, 171/22.

comown, adj., *common*, 147/21.

companʒeoun, n., *companion*, 21/7.

compleiss, v., *please, satisfy*, 89/22.

componyng, vbl. n., *coming to an agreement*, 87/1.

compromit, n., *agreement*, 143/19, 147/1, 147/3 etc.

comptit, p.p. adj., *counted, reckoned*, 153/10.

comunis, n. pl., *common people*, 25/27.

concluid, v., *decide*, 19/11, 39/18.

concurrantis, n., *assistance*, 53/20 [Earliest example in DOST 1564, but e.m.E. from 1525].

concurrence, n., *opportunity, occasion*, 37/23, 37/28, 39/2. [This sense not in DOST].

condiscend, v., *enter into particulars*, 67/23.

conducit, pret., *led*, 29/13, 37/5.

conducing, vbl. n., *leading, conducting*, 29/15, 31/25, 33/12.

confideratioun, n., *alliance*, 37/6, 53/7.

conforme, adj., *corresponding*, 9/18, 17/12, 19/25 etc.

conformelie, adv., *in conformity with*, 61/10.
conquess, v., *conquer*, 73/21.
conqueiss, n., *conquest*, 81/5; **conquesis**, 83/18.
consauit, pret., *formed in the mind, conceived*, 37/19.
consequenter, adv., *consequently*, 61/14, 111/11, 137/25.
constrane, v., *force*, 37/16.
consuetud, n., *custom, habit*, 169/13.
contemptioun, n., *contempt*, 17/1.
contempnyng, n., *contempt*, 35/18.
contenand, pres. p. adj., *containing*, 13/6.
contenit, p.p. adj., *contained*, 7/1, 9/3, 15/14.
continente, n., *contents*, 9/10 [Not in DOST].
continew, v., *delay, postpone*, 55/1, 129/24; *continue*, **continuew**, 53/2;
   continewis, pres., 15/11.
continewalie, adv., *continually*, 31/26, 45/14, 65/4.
continewall, adj., *continuous*, 65/10.
contrar, n., *opposite*, 35/21.
contrewit, p.p. adj., *invented*, 135/3. [This form not in DOST].
convenit, pret., *called together*, 159/1.
convoying, vbl. n., *carrying*, 23/20.
coronat, p.p. adj., *crowned*, 107/4; **coronate**, 149/7.
countra man, n., *neighbour, countryman*, 3/3, 29/10; **contray man**, 9/4;
   countray man, 45/3, 111/22; **countrey man**, 83/8.
courticianis, n. pl., *courtiers*, 25/6; **courtisianis**, 163/13.
cousing, n., *cousin*, 25/3.
crewell, adj., *cruel*, 47/11.
craw, n., *crow*, 133/1.
culd, pret., *could*, 25/16, 53/16.
cullerand, pres. p. adj., *disguising, explaining away*, 121/19.
culpabill, adj., *culpable*, 13/16.
cuming, vbl. n., *coming*, 39/7.
cuming, p.p. adj., *come*, 7/12, 29/3.
cumit, p.p. adj., *come*, 43/5.
curage, n., *courage*, 29/8.

D

debilitate, p.p. adj., *enfeebled*, 41/27. [Earliest example in DOST 1557;
   e.m.E. 1552].

decase, *fall,* 111/13. [OF decasser]. [Not in DOST].

deceiss, n., *death,* 79/18, 87/1, 87/25 etc.

decern v., *decide,* 169/7, 169/10; **decerne,** 171/3.

decesioun, n., *decision,* 19/3.

deducit, p.p. adj., *reduced, deducted* 155/1.

deif, adj., *deaf,* 141/22.

delatrice, n., *accuser,* 41/4. [L. delatrix]. [Not in DOST; cf. *delation,* attested from 1550].

delyure, v., *deliver,* 129/15.

deming, vbl. n., *judgment,* 57/20.

deponit, p.p. adj., *deposed,* 87/9. [L. deponere].

destitude, adj., *lacking, devoid,* 113/1.

detenit, pret., *kept in custody,* 23/3; **detint,** p.p. adj., 23/24; **detenit,** p.p. adj., *withheld,* 167/4.

detenyng, vbl. n., *keeping in custody,* 31/14; **deteyning,** 31/19; **detining,** 25/3.

detractit, pret., *avoided,* 151/24.

deturne, v., *diverge,* 31/3. [Earliest example in DOST Hamilton; but e.m.E. before 1450].

deulie, adv., *properly,* 17/22.

deutie, n., *duty, obligation,* 29/18; **dewitey,** 85/3, 155/4; **dewitie,** 141/15, 151/24.

devidit, pret., *divided,* 149/18.

difficile, adj., *difficult,* 73/26 [OF difficile].

diffine, v., *define,* 19/11.

diffinitiue, adj., *conclusive,* 19/7, 155/15.

dilugit, n., *flood,* 63/25. [This form not in DOST].

disapoynt, v., *cancel,* 35/18; **disapoyntit,** pret., 43/4; p.p. adj., 161/27, 167/2.

disapoynting, vbl. n., *cancellation,* 15/20, 37/4.

disappunctit, p.p. adj., *cancelled,* 39/13; **disapunctit,** 41/17.

disburdonit, p.p. adj., *relieved of a burden,* 41/23.

disburijt, p.p. adj., *exhumed,* 171/10.

diserine, v., ?*discern,* 63/2.

disherist, p.p. adj., *disinherited,* 35/9.

dochtir, n., *daughter,* 21/14, 23/27, 71/1 etc.

domesticall, adj., *internal,* 155/14; **domistical,** 19/10. [Earliest example in DOST Winȝet 1562/3].

dois, v., *does,* 13/16.

doubtabill, adj., *uncertain, doubtful,* 19/4.

doutit, p.p. adj., *feared*, 159/4.
doutsum, adj., *doubtful*, 75/8.
dow, adj., *due*, 111/14.
draif, pret., *drove*, 27/28.
dredour, n., *fear*, 43/20.
dreid, v., *be afraid*, 131/16.
dreiding, vbl. n., *dreading*, 113/1.
drevin, p.p. adj., *driven*, 23/22.
duik, n., *duke,* ·31/5.
.**durris**, n. pl., *doors*, 65/19.

E

effectionat, *see* **affectionat**.
efferis, v., *is appropriate to*, 169/7.
eftir, prep., *after*, 77/3.
eiectit, p.p. adj., *cast out*, 89/14, 89/16, 121/2 etc. [Not in DOST; earliest example in OED 1555].
elikwyiss, adv., *similarly*, 81/3.
ellevin, num., *eleven*, 81/1.
empeschit, p.p. adj., *prevented, hindered*, 43/2.
entirit, p.p. adj., *commenced*, 51/24.
entres, n., *entrance*, 33/6.
eschaip, v., *escape*, 143/17.
eschame, v., *be ashamed*, 3/8; **eschamit**, p.p. adj., 3/11.
euerilk, adj., *every*, 21/12, 79/17.
evacuation, n., *purging, refutation*, 167/2. [This sense not in DOST; earliest example of this sense in OED 1650].
evident, n., *piece of evidence, document*, 45/21, 47/5, 163/16 etc.
except, v., *plead as an objection*, 19/10.
excessius, adj., *excessive*, 167/15. [Not in DOST].
excusatorijs, adj. pl., *excusatory*, 25/8. [Earliest example in DOST 1577; but e.m.E. from 1535].
executit, p.p. adj., *carried out*, 43/15.
executouris, n. pl., *executors*, 25/21, 79/17.
expreme, v., *express*, 143/23.
extractioun, n., *making of an extract*, 137/18, 137/23. [Not in DOST; this sense not recorded in OED before 1656].
extractit, p.p. adj., *extracted*, 137/19.

F

facill, adj., *readily yielding to persuasion*, 53/13, 57/12, 145/19.
falit, pret., *failed*, 85/3; p.p. adj., 105/25, 107/13.
fallowschip, n., *company*, 3/7.
fand, pret., *found*, 23/11, 75/22.
fassoun, n., *fashion*, 41/23.
fealteis, n. pl., *oaths, fealties*, 131/6, 131/11.
fedelite, m., *fealty*, 135/15.
ferd, num., *fourth*, 7/15, 23/12, 25/4 etc.
ferder, adv., *further*, 55/1, 73/28, 77/5 etc; **ferdar**, 29/10; **ferther**, 41/12.
fluid, n., *river*, 37/7.
fochin, p.p. adj., *fought*, 81/19.
foir-saying, vbl. n., *above statement*, 83/24. [Not in DOST].
for, num., *four*, 105/20.
fordwart, adv., *forward*, 21/7, 53/26.
force, n., *necessity*, 101/1. [Its use without a preposition is found in both Rolland and Lauder].
forder, adv., *further*, 69/23, 79/24, 85/20 etc.
formale, adv., *in proper style*, 139/25, 143/4, 167/24.
fra, prep., conj., *from*, 7/12, 23/11, 31/4 etc.
fred, p.p. adj., *freed*, 23/24.
freslie, adv., *freshly*, 17/3.
freuole, adj., *frivolous, of little account*, 67/1.
fund, p.p. adj., *found*, 63/12.
furneiss, v., *provide*, 51/14.
furnissing, vbl. n., *supplying*, 37/11.
fyif, num., *five*, 7/19.
fyift, num., *fifth*, 7/17, 33/4, 49/20 etc.; **fyft**, 29/9.
fyn, n., *end*.

G

garnesoun, n., *garrison*, 49/7, 51/15.
gayis, v., *goes*, 171/8.
geif, v., *give*, 13/18; **gaif**, pret., 107/8; **gaiff**, 121/5; **geifand**, pres. p., 47/9.
generale, adv., *generally*, 83/12.
gevar, n., *giver*, 169/2.

gevin, vbl. n., *giving*, 19/16.
gife, conj., *if*, 11/6, 15/15, 39/19 etc.; **giffe**, 17/14, 125/11; **giff**, 109/6;
 giue, 51/26; **give**, 37/17.
graif, adj., *solemn*, 11/3.
gratuiteis, n. pl., *favours*, 53/24.
grauitie, n., *solemn bearing*, 13/9.
greit, adj., *great*, 7/23, 9/8; **Greitt**, 33/17; **grit**, 19/3.
ground, n., *land*, 17/2; *basis*, 155/23; **groundis**, pl., 151/22.
guid, adj., *good*, 3/13, 13/2, 13/5 etc.; **gude**, 13/11.
guidis, n. pl., *goods*, 27/28, 49/1.
guidlie, adj., *goodly*, 39/23; adv., *well*, 15/12.
guid-brothir, n., *brother-in-law*, 27/10, 27/22, 29/5 etc.; **guid-brethir**,
 91/10.
guid-sone, n., *son-in-law*, 23/25, 25/9.
gyd, v., *lead*, 31/22; **gydit**, pret., 63/6.

H

haif, v., *have*, 5/11, 7/12, 13/8 etc.; **haifand**, pres. p., 33/6, 37/6, 37/10
 etc.; **haifing**, 37/8.
haill, adj., *whole*, 59/6, 149/18.
hald, n., *stronghold*, 23/8; **haldis**, pl., 31/8.
hald, v., *hold*, 13/17, 139/1; **haldin**, p.p. adj., 31/10; *been kept*, 39/20.
handill, v., *treat*, 125/22; **handillit**, p.p. adj., 49/12. 139/26.
hant, v., *frequent*, 169/15; **hantit**, pret., 13/8.
hard, pret., *heard*, 13/12, 29/19.
hartlie, adj., *sincere*, 27/11; **hertlie**, 37/25.
he, adj., *high*, 29/8.
hear, adj., *higher*, 13/17.
heding, vbl. n., *beheading*, 41/10.
heir, v., *hear*, 15/1.
heid, n., *head*, 23/11; **heid toun**, n., *capital*, 37/15. [Not in DOST, but cf.
 hede burgh].
heretrice, n., *heiress*, 9/1, 35/2, 99/1 etc. [OF heretrice, L heretrix].
hethand, adj., *pagan, heathen*, 165/9. [This form not in DOST].
hiddouis, adj., *hideous*, 37/11.
historiante, n., *circle of historians*, 75/8. [Not in DOST].
historiciane, n., *historian*, 57/1, 57/7, 125/16 etc.

horss, n. pl., *horses*, 125/2.

hosill, adj., *hostile*, 39/22. [This form not in DOST].

hostage, n., *hostelry*, 131/3. [Earliest example in DOST Rolland; e.m.E. from 1547 but cf. *ostage*].

howbeit, conj., *although*, 13/8, 23/7, 69/18 etc.

hundreth, num., *hundred*, 5/12, 5/19, 13/14.

I

ile, n., *island*, 59/1, 61/5, 61/24 etc.

ilk, adj., *each, every*, 77/3, 167/10; *same*, 83/2.

Imperatrice, n., *Empress*, 91/12.

impeschit, p.p. adj., *obstructed*, 37/11.

impire, n., *empire, rule*, 71/10.

improbatioun, n., *disproof*, 19/19 (*see note*).

improvis, v., *disproves*, 101/3; **improvin**, p.p. adj., 79/29, 109/21. [Earliest example in DOST Hamilton; but e.m.E. from 1489].

impruif, v., *disprove*, 51/1; **impruife**, 75/20.

impugnatioun, n., *objection*, 69/4, 93/17, 115/24 etc. [Not in DOST; but cf. *impugnment*, attested from 1549; *impugnacion* in late ME].

impung, v., *question, object to*, 57/5, 57/7; **impugnit**, p.p. adj., 163/2; **impugnate**, 111/5.

incommodite, n., *inconvenience*, 35/16.

incontinent, adv., *without delay*, 31/5, 33/4, 47/2 etc.

incresche, v., *increase*, 169/23.

induce, v., *bring in, introduce*, 159/27; **inducit**, p.p. adj., 103/15.

inductioun, n., *inducement*, 41/17.

induring, vbl. n., *duration*, 117/5, 119/12. [This sense not in DOST; *enduring* as vbl. n. found only in Hay].

inextingguabill, adj., *inextinguishable*, 67/1.

inextinguissabill, adj., *inextinguishable*, 41/24, 67/1. [Not in DOST but e.m.E. from 1509; cf. *inextinguibill*].

infamite, n., *infamy*, 65/13.

inime, n., *enemy*, 73/22.

iniust, adj., *unjust*, 17/16, 51/22, 67/2.

instant, adj., *current*, 5/13, 13/7.

intercommown, v., *consult, have dealings with*, 39/16.

interpryss, n., *undertaking*, 39/14.

interpryss, v., *undertake*, 39/14.

interrupit, p.p. adj., *interrupted*, 43/1.
interspace, n., *space between*, 93/15. [Not in DOST; but late ME found *c*.1420].
interteinit, pret., *entertained*, 43/23; **intertenijt**, 123/14.
intret, pret., *entered*, 15/7.
inuiolate, p.p. adj., *inviolate*, 45/11.
inwart, adj., *interior*, 43/11.
irksum, adj., *wearying*, 15/4.

J

joyit, pret., *enjoyed*, 123/15.
joysance, n., *enjoyment*, 117/13. [OF jouissance]. [Not in DOST, but e.m.E. from Caxton 1483].
just, adj., *rightful*, 7/5; iust, 7/3; *accurate*, 97/4.

K

ken, v., *know*, 149/16.
kest, v., *cast*, 159/13.
knawlege, n., *knowledge*, 9/8.
knawlege, v., *acknowledge*, 95/20.
ky, n. pl., *cattle*, 125/2.

L

lacerate, p.p. adj., *torn, torn up*, 153/2. [Earliest example in DOST 1614, but e.m.E. from 1542].
laik, v., *lack*, 97/20.
laith, adj., *loath, unwilling*, 95/20.
langar, adj., *longer*, 33/15, 51/28, 159/28.
lauthfull, adj., *lawful*, 67/12; **lauchfull**, 119/19.
leag, n., *league, alliance*, 23/26, 31/2; **leagis**, pl., 49/4.
leid, n., *language*, 11/7, 61/16.
leif, v., *leave*, 127/16.
leir, v., *learn*, 63/5.
leirnit, p.p. adj., *learned, educated*, 21/6.

leud, adj., *vulgar, illiterate*, 43/15.
leuear, n., *liver*, 33/16, 51/28, 159/28.
levit, pret., *lived*, 119/4.
liniell, adj., *in the direct line*, 113/1.
list, v., *choose, please*, 133/12.
liturate, adj., *learned*, 57/6.
lovable, adj., *?legal*, 137/13.
luge, v., *lodge*, 131/2.
lugeing, vbl. n., *lodging*, 131/1.
lyf, n., *life*; **on lyf**, *alive*, 3/13.
lyk, adj., *probable*, 101/4.

M

ma, adj., *more*, 59/5, 59/13, 61/4 etc.
mair, adj., *more*, 13/10, 27/11, 37/14 etc; **moir**, 163/13.
mairattoure, conj., *moreover*, 83/8.
mairoure, conj., *moreover*, 69/26.
maiestate, n., *majesty*, 7/11. [DOST gives as a nonce variant of *majeste*, from Gau].
maistiris, n. pl., *sirs*, 131/3.
mak, v., *make*, 7/9; **maikis**, pres., 13/9.
man, v., *must*, 63/18, 97/3, 105/22 etc. [ON man].
mantene, v., *uphold*, 15/12, 29/12, 31/26 etc; **mantenit**, p.p. adj., *supported*, 23/3.
mantening, vbl. n., *support*, 29/15; **mantenyng**, 33/8.
marchis, n. pl., *borders*, 7/17, 69/16, 83/7; **merchis**, 45/19.
mater, n., *subject*, 35/20.
maturalie, adv., *with due deliberation*, 17/25.
meinȝeonis, *see* **minȝeonis**.
mekill, adj., *much*, 5/2, 11/6, 13/13 etc.
mene, v., *intend, convey*, 45/5; **menis**, pres., 147/23; **menit**, pret., 39/3, p.p. adj., 35/23.
merchis, *see* **marchis**.
merwell, v., *wonder*, 55/24; **merualat**, pret., 49/5; **merwalat**, p.p. adj., 149/9.
ministrat, p.p. adj., *provided*, 155/7. [Earliest example of this sense in DOST 1565].
minȝeonis, n. pl., *favourites*, 89/21; **meinȝeonis**, 41/18; **munȝeonis**, 171/13.

miseiss, n., *distress*, 7/11.
misgyding, vbl. n., *misrule*, 5/3.
mishaving, vbl. n., *misbehaviour*, 5/3.
misknaw, v., *be ignorant*, 149/22.
misordourit, p.p. adj., *irregular*, 19/18, 19/24, 19/26.
moir, *see* **mair**.
mone, v., *must*, 69/1, 101/2, 111/7 etc.
moneth, n., *month*, 5/14, 15/9; **monethis**, pl., 91/23.
mony, adj., *many*, 13/14, 29/1.
moving, pres. p., *concerning*, 9/5.
movit, pret., *instituted*, 47/10, 57/13; *moved*, 53/22.
munʒeonis, *see* **minʒeonis**.
mynd, v., *intend*, 49/20, 149/21, 151/1; **myndit**, pret., 21/15, 73/25; p.p. adj., 155/5.

N

na, adj., *no*, 27/30, 51/6.
nebour, n., *neighbour*, 19/1, 25/17.
necessarlie, adv., *necessarily*, 79/16, 83/19, 97/7 etc.
necesser, adj., *necessary*, 61/5.
necligentlie, adv., *negligently*, 93/3.
neir, adj., *near*, 157/2.
nemmit, adj., *(above) named*, 165/11.
nepot, n., *nephew*, 29/21, 33/5, 33/18 etc; **nepote**, 33/16, 93/23, 123/7; **nepotis**, pl., 39/24.
nerrast, adv., *nearest*, 27/15, 69/25, 89/19.
nerther, adv., *nearer*, 155/25. [This form not in DOST].
newtrale, adj., *neutral*, 113/18.
nichtbour, n., *neighbour*, 25/11, 55/8, 59/10 etc; **nychtbour**, 11/4, 17/8, 41/5 etc.
nixt, adj., *next*, 105/15.
nobill, adj., *noble*, 9/1.
nocht, adv., *not*, 7/9, 11/4, 21/2 etc.
nor, conj., *than*, 33/11, 83/23
not, v., *accuse*, 45/4.
notaris, n. poss., *notary's*, 139/5, 165/25.
notour, adj., *notorious*,
notourlie, adv., *notoriously*, 39/8, 49/17.

nouther, adv., conj., *neither*, 79/24, 85/27, 123/4 etc.; **nother**, 79/21, 103/17, 127/10; **nothir**, 9/15, 19/3, 29/16 etc.; **nouthir**, 39/23, 93/2, 129/21.
novatioun, n., *innovation*, 53/5; **novationis**, pl., 39/6.
noy, v., *annoy*, 33/1.
nummer, n., *number*, 109/16; **numeris**, pl., 105/21.

O

oblising, n., *contract, obligation*, 9/2.
obseruance, n., *observance, loyalty*, 41/21.
ocht, n., *anything*, 53/22.
occurantis, n. pl., *events*, 53/19.
omage, n., *homage*, 93/13.
onderstand, v., *understand*, 21/2; **onderstandis**, pres., 11/7.
ony, pron., adv., *any*, 9/4, 11/7, 33/12 etc.
or, conj., *before*, 27/26, 73/18, 73/22 etc.
or, conj., *or.*, 9/4, 25/21, 31/22, etc.
ordanit, p.p. adj., *laid down*, 145/8.
ordinarie, adj., *regular*, 155/10.
ordourlie, adv., *regularly, properly*, 19/2.
our, adv., *excessively*, 83/12.
our, prep., *above, over*, 167/17.
outher, adv., *either*, 79/1; **outhir**, 67/14, 137/16.
outlandismen, n. pl., *foreigners, strangers*, 43/20.
outlay-maen, n. pl., *outlaws*, 45/4. [?The result of confusion with *outlaw*].
outpassing, vbl. n., *departure*, 153/23.

P

parkit, p.p. adj., *encamped*, 37/10.
peceablie, adv., *peacefully*, 87/24.
peopill, n. pl., *people* 3/15, 57/25, 63/17; **peopillis**, pl. poss., 63/2.
peraduentour, adv., *perhaps*, 25/21, 87/14.
periure, n., *perjury*, 41/5.
persaue, v., *observe, apprehend*, 5/11; **persawand**, pres. p., 53/1.
persequutit, p.p. adj., *persecuted*, 53/14.

persequutioun, n., *persecution*, 171/18.
personage, n., ?*dignity*, 29/18.
pertene, v., *belong*, 119/25; **pertenis**, pres., *is appropriate*, 169/4.
pleable, adj., *suitable for litigation*, 143/8, 155/10.
pleisour, n., *pleasure, wish*, 3/3.
posseid, v., *possess*, 61/1; **possedit**, p.p. adj., 87/4.
posterite, n., *descendants*, 59/16; **posteritie**, 21/16.
potent, adj., *mighty*, 19/5, 113/7; *legitimate*, 89/19.
practizate, pret., *contrived*, 133/3.
prechouris, n. pl., *preachers*, 45/9.
preif, n., *proof*, 27/23.
preif, v., *prove*, 15/20, 131/14.
prent, n., *edition*, 67/7.
prentare, n., *printer*, 105/25.
prentit, pret., *printed*, 17/22; p.p. adj., 5/19, 107/1.
preparatiue, n., *preparation*, 51/18.
preposter, adj., *preposterous*, 101/12. [Not otherwise recorded in MSc.].
prescriptable, adj., *subject to a limitation of time*, 155/1.
prescriptioun, n., *expiry of a limitation of time*, 153/26, 153/28.
pretendit, p.p. adj., *claimed*, 119/2.
prevalie, adv., *privately, secretly*, 39/3, 41/18; **preuale**, 137/17.
prevate, adj., *private, secret*, 51/4, 119/5; **prevat**, 119/5; **preuate**, 137/17.
prevay, adj., *private*; **Prevay Chalmer**, *Privy Chamber*, 35/24.
probatioun, n., *proof*, 55/23, 69/3, 77/6 etc.
procedit, p.p. adj., *proceeded with*, 17/10, 19/2, 113/26.
process, n., *legal procedure*, 19/3.
propirtie, n., *property*, 113/25.
propone, v., *set forth*, 19/9; **proponit**, p.p. adj., 17/6.
proponyng, vbl. n., *putting forward (of a plea or statement)*, 19/15, 111/16.
proportis, v. pres., *expresses, states*, 23/27, 27/25.
propreitie, n., *ownership*, 127/7, 127/15, 129/21; **propriete**, 125/5.
proprietare, adj., *having in ownership*, 123/15. [Not otherwise recorded in MSc.; in e.m.E. from 1589].
provitioun, n., *Providence*, 63/21.
pruif, n., *proof*, 31/16, 33/12, 47/14 etc.; **pruife**, 19/11, 95/17; **prufe**, 43/16.
pruife, v., *prove*, 15/13, 49/9, 57/2 etc.; **proif**, 89/24.
publist, p.p. adj., *published*, 5/17, 9/7, 15/15.
puissant, adj., *powerful*, 5/15. [Earliest recorded example of this form in MSc.].

puissantlie, adv., *powerfully, effectively*, 39/1.
pupill, n., *minor under fourteen years of age*, 123/2.

Q

quha, pron., *who*, 27/14, 29/19, 33/18 etc.
quhais, pron., *whose*, 63/15; **quhayis**, 39/22.
quhar, conj., adv., *where*, 3/3, 19/13, 23/10 etc.; *in which*, 39/10.
quharat, adv., *at which*, 49/5.
quharof, adv., *of which*, 21/11, 25/28.
quharwith, adv., *with which*, 5/5.
quhat, pron., adj., *what*, 29/15, 35/5.
quhayis, *see* **quhais**.
quhen, adv., conj., *when*, 9/13.
quheit, n., *whit*, 53/22.
quheir, conj., *where*, 129/4.
quhene, adj., *few*, 121/13.
quhiddir, conj., *whether*, 59/20.
quhilk, pron., *which, who, whom*, 5/18, 5/20, 7/22 etc.
quhilkis, pl. pron., *which*, 7/5, 35/8.
quhill, conj., prep., *until*, 3/12, 87/25, 99/2 etc.
quhithir, conj., *whether*, 9/17, 75/9, 139/3; **quhiddir**, 59/20.
quhithir, pron., *which (of two)*, 13/15, 61/9.
quhombe, pron., *by whom*, 157/7.
quhomto, pron., *to whom*, 99/6.
quhomwith, pron., *with whom*, 113/12.
quhon, adj., conj., *when*, 51/24, 53/5; **quhone**, 35/13, 113/16.
quhy, adv., *why*, 53/20, 103/6.
quhy, n., *reason*, 3/10.
quhytt, adj., *white*, 133/2.

R

radis, n. pl., *raids*, 51/5; **raiddis**, 51/17.
raiss, pret., *rose*, 53/15, 91/9.
rander, v., *give, give up*, 45/1.
randering, vbl. n., *giving up*, 15/21, 45/3; **rendering**, 7/9.

rang, *see* **ringne**.
reageing, pres. p, *raging*, 31/12.
reasown, v., *reason, argue*, 15/1.
recognoscit, p.p. adj., *acknowledged*, 55/12.
recuilȝeit, pret., *gathered together, harboured*, 81/15. [Earliest recorded example in MSc. but in e.m.E. from Caxton].
refewing, vbl. n., *refutation*, 111/11, 167/4. [Not otherwise recorded].
refuiss, v., *refuse*, 37/2.
registreis, n. pl., *registers*, 17/5, 55/24, 139/25 etc.
regne, v., *reign*, 67/19; **regnit**, pret., 71/8, 169/16.
reid, v., *read*, 19/21; p.p. adj., 5/11, 15/11, 15/16 etc.; **red**, 5/16, 15/19.
reherss, n., *recital*, 155/18.
reherss, v., *repeat*, 35/7; **rehersit**, p.p. adj., 35/1.
reknit, p.p. adj., *counted, considered*, 105/12.
remanand, pres. p., *remaining*, 23/18, 27/22.
reparit, pret., *resorted*, 29/17.
repellit, p.p. adj., *repelled*, 113/8, 113/12.
reput, v., *believe*, 51/26, 55/9; **repute**, p.p. adj., 53/9, 65/8, 163/28; **reputis**, pres., 163/11.
requisitioun, n., *demand*, 165/12.
resaif, v., *receive*, 75/14; **resauit**,
resingne, v., *resign*, 121/11.
restorance, n., *returning*, 45/22.
restrikit, p.p. adj., *limited*, 49/18.
reule, n., *rule, government*, 47/20, 49/15.
reulis, v. pres., *rules*, 59/17.
reulare, n., *ruler*, 61/8; **reullaris**, pl., 59/1, 61/4, 61/24; **reularis**, 61/14.
riale, adj., *royal*, 29/14, 31/25, 35/1; **reale**, 33/13; **ryale**, 41/11.
ringne, v., *reign*, 31/22, 35/5, 41/9 etc.; **rang**, pret., 87/24, 89/20; **rangne**, 93/7.
roulkis, n. pl., *(meaning uncertain)*, 55/20.
rub, v., *rob*, 43/21.
ruffill, v., *bring into disorder, confuse*, 3/15, 5/2.
ruid, adj., *common*, 57/25.
rute, n., *root*, 21/18, 25/12.
ryding, vbl. n., *riding, raid*, 51/3, 51/9.
ryiss, v., *rise*, 113/2.
rynnis, v. pres., *runs*, 155/26.

S

sa, adv., conj., *so*, 59/3, 81/25, 83/10 etc.
saciate, p.p. adj., *satisfied*, 45/6.
saffete, n., *safety*, 45/10.
sait, n., *seat*; Apostolic Sait, *the Holy See*, 41/22.
salbe, v., *shall be*, 61/17.
saldin, adv., *seldom*, 33/23.
sam, adj., *same*, 3/7, 7/14, 9/2 etc.
samyn, adj., *same*, 15/17, 19/11, 23/11 etc.
satefie, v., *satisfy*, 165/3.
sauflie, adv., *safely*, 29/13.
sauftie, n., *safety*, 129/12.
sauite, n, *safety*, 129/17.
sax, num., *six*, 9/2, 31/8, 59/23; *sixth*, 7/21.
saxt, num., *sixth*, 17/6, 69/13, 73/1; **sext**, 71/13.
schak, n., *shaking*, 81/12, 87/9.
schamit, pret., *ashamed*, 39/23.
schaw, v., *show*, 103/6; **schew**, 37/1; pret., 53/3, 53/13, 59/16, etc.
scheddin, vbl. n., *shedding*, 45/7.
schir, n., *sir*, 13/5; **schirris**, pl., 13/2, 15/16; **schiris**, 15/6.
scho, pron., *she*, 25/16, 133/2.
se, v., *see*, 19/15; **seand**, pres. p., 37/12, 111/26; *see also* **sey**.
seid, n., *seed*, 35/4.
seill, n., *seal*, 7/23; **selis**, pl., 131/9, 131/15.
sein3eouris, n. pl., *lordships*, 119/5.
seir, adj., *very*, 35/1.
self, adj., *same*, 25/12, 155/15.
semblable, adj., *similar*, 51/23, 161/11, 167/17.
sembleablie, adv., *similarly*, 87/11.
semit, pret., *was appropriate*, 39/13.
sen, conj., *since*, 7/21, 47/6, 89/2 etc.
send, pret., *sent*, 31/5, 35/14, 35/21 etc.; p.p. adj., 53/6.
sen-syn, adv., *since*, 155/25.
senschence, adv., *since*, 153/8.
seuerit, p.p. adj., *cut off*, 39/16.
sevint, num., *seventh*, 21/19, 23/4.
sey, n., *sea*, 37/12, 65/4, 65/11; **se**, 23/21.
sic, adj., *such*, 27/1, 35/3, 35/4 etc.; **sick**, 15/3, 35/3, 35/22 etc.
siclik, adv., *similarly*, 47/21, 77/17; **siclyk**, 69/3.

sikand, pres. p., *seeking*, 161/26.

sindlare, adv., *seldom*, 35/1. [This form not otherwise found in MSc.].

sindre, adj., *various*, 23/25, 25/6, 27/2 etc.

sistir-sone, n., *nephew, sister's son*, 27/14; **sistir-sonis**, poss., 31/8.

skoupit, p.p. adj., *erred*, 79/1.

slauchtir, n., *killing*, 17/1, 23/7.

slippit, p.p. adj., *omitted*, 83/15, 93/17.

slumberit, p.p. adj., *slept*, 97/16.

smuke, n., *smoke*, 65/26.

sobir, adj., *small, little*, 45/23, 47/1, 47/11 etc.

socht, pret., *sought*, 31/20.

solemplie, adv., *solemnly*, 125/12.

solempnit, p.p. adj., *solemn*, 141/4, 143/14.

solempnizing, vbl. n., *enactment*, 103/19.

solistatioun, n., *request, soliciting*, 53/17.

solistit, pret., *requested*, 39/3; p.p. adj., 35/22.

sonare, adv.m., *more quickly, sooner*, 63/16.

sone, adv., *soon*, 5/6.

sone, n., *sun*, 7/3.

sone, n., *son*, 23/5.

speciale, adv., *specially*, 71/9.

specifeit, p.p. adj., *specified*, 43/9, 69/7; **specifeand**, pres. p., 139/3.

speir, v., *ask*, 47/3, 59/16, 59/20 etc.; **speris**, pres., 3/5; **sperit**, p.p. adj., 61/16.

sponsit, p.p. adj., *married*, 41/10.

spuilȝe, n., *loot*, 35/9; **spuilȝeis**, pl., 49/26, 51/3, 51/5 etc.

spuilȝeit, pret., *despoiled, looted*, 49/4, 49/25.

stabill, v., *establish*, 61/13; **stabillit**, pp. adj., 71/16.

stabillisment, n., *establishment*, 111/14.

stall, pret., *stole*, 133/10.

stane, n., *stone*, 29/8, 163/15.

starklie, adv., *strongly, powerfully*, 37/10.

steill, v., *steal*, 133/4; **stall**, pret., 133/10.

stok, n., *stock*, 33/22, 33/25, 35/3 etc.

stomocate, adj., *angry*, 53/1.

stop, n., *prevention*, 25/18.

stormested, p.p. adj., *storm-bound*, 25/1.

straik, n., *stroke, blow*, 81/12, 87/9.

stranglie, adj., *strong*, 37/9.

stryif, n., *strife*, 31/11.

strynth, n., *strength*, 139/1.
stuid, pret., *stood*, 35/7.
subdittis, n. pl., *subjects*, 45/7.
sueir, v., *swear*, 83/11.
suirlie, adv., *surely*, 39/2, 97/17.
supponit, pret., *supposed*, 113/14.
surrenderence, n., *surrender*, 125/16, 127/10.
suyth, n., *truth*, 59/19, 73/20.
swa, adj., conj., *so*, 9/14, 71/14, 79/26 etc.; **sua**, 73/17.
swerd, n., *sword*, 81/13, 87/10.
syn, adv., *later, afterwards*, 59/6, 97/12, 147/26; **syne**, 31/1.

T

taikin, n., *token*, 25/15.
talkin, vbl. n., *capture, taking*, 51/19.
tane, p.p. adj., *taken*, 25/26, 129/12, 161/3.
techeraris, n. pl., *teachers*, 45/9.
tennour, n., *content, sense*, 133/22, 135/5, 137/7.
tent, num., *tenth*, 85/20, 89/1, 89/12.
testefeit, p.p. adj., *sworn*, 149/14.
tha, adj., *those*, 89/18, 113/7.
than, adv., *then*, 11/12.
thesaurie, n., *treasury*, 133/4, 141/24, 165/5.
thir, adj., *these*, 9/4, 13/18, 29/3.
thirlage, n., *bondage*, 91/6, 165/2.
thraw, v., *throw*, 5/4.
threttein, num., *thirteen*, 95/18.
threttie, num., *thirty*, 61/19, 77/13.
thrid, num., *third*, 7/11, 139/24; **thride**, 13/4.
tiranfull, adj., *tyrannical, oppressive*, 147/22.
titill, n., *title, claim*, 37/21, 59/20, 61/2 etc.
titter, adv., *rather*, 63/9.
tractat, n., *treatise*, 5/16; **tractatis**, pl., 15/14, 15/17, 17/9.
traffict, v., *trade, have dealings with*, 171/5, 171/16; **traffictit**, pret., 171/6.
    [Earliest recorded occurrence in MSc.].
traistit, pret., *trusted*, 33/20.
trasoun, n., *treason*, 45/14.
trastie, adj., *trusty*, 3/14.

tretable, adj., *tractable*, 53/2.
trewis, n., *truce*, 51/11.
truffill, adj., *trivial*, 163/1.
tuelf, num., *twelfth*, 81/21, 95/17.
tuo, num., *two*, 31/13.
tutour, n., *guardian*, 159/5.
tuyss, adv., *twice*, 61/21; **tuyiss**, 123/7.
twa, num., *two*, 5/12, 13/6, 13/15 etc.; *tway*, 15/20.
tym, n., *time*, 7/14.

þ

þai, pron., *they*, 5/9; **thai**, 19/21.
þair, adv., *there*, 31/6.
þam, pron., *them*, 9/4; **þame**, 9/12, 9/17, 15/18 etc.
þir, adj., *these*, 3/8, 11/6.

V

vaiage, n., *journey*, 55/3.
vaillieant, adj., *valiant*, 81/9.
vaignes, n. pl., *tricks*, 125/22 (*see note*).
vait, n., *wait*; **in a vait**, *in waiting*, 31/27; **one a vait**, 159/25.
valeur, adj., *valid*, 119/19.
valour, n., *value*, 47/2, 47/12, 55/10; **valeur**, 127/12.
verisimile, adj., *probable*, 81/9.
vertuis, adj., *virtuous*, 81/10.
vesiyng, vbl. n., *seeing*, 61/21.
vikit, adj., *wicked*, 43/18.
vincust, pret., *defeated*, 69/15, 77/20, 85/8 etc.
vnaffectionat, adj., *unbiased*, 5/9.
vnit, p.p. adj., *joined, united*, 59/1, 59/19, 65/5 etc.
vnkyndlie, adj., *unnatural*, 29/7.
vnlawis, n. pl., *fines*, 25/26.
vnpassabill, adj., *not able to be crossed*, 37/7.
vnpleisand, adj., *unpleasant*, 91/6.
vsis, v. pres., *is accustomed*, 51/4, 125/1; **vsit**, p.p. adj., *employed*, 29/19.
vodit, p.p. adj., *emptied*, 161/21.

vthir, adj., *other*, 5/16, 11/7, 13/3 etc.
vther-wayiss, adv., *otherwise*, 123/6.
vtwart, adj., ?*perverse*, 129/1.

W

waikit, p.p. adj., *weakened*, 41/27.
waiklie, adv., *weakly*, 49/12, 77/23, 165/26.
waisting, vbl. n., *laying waste*, 51/18.
wald, v., *would*, 7/8, 29/6, 71/22.
walkin, v., *awaken, commence*, 53/21.
wand, n., *branch, stick*, 5/4.
warald, n., *world*, 65/10.
wardill, n., *world*, 39/27, 169/21.
wardlie, adj., *worldly*, 135/18.
warlie, adv., *cautiously*, 45/3.
wechtie, adj., *serious, weighty*, 19/4, 19/6, 69/1 etc.
weichtiar, adj., *more serious, weightier*, 13/17.
weill, adv., *well*, 29/16.
weir, n., *war*, 5/7, 5/13, 7/2 etc.; **weiris**, pl., 13/13, 17/16.
weir, v., *make war*, 33/5.
weirfair, n., *warfare*, 5/6, 31/23; **veirfare**, 5/3.
weirmen, n. pl., *warriors, soldiers*, 31/6.
weschell, n., *vessel*, 37/8.
wrang, n., *wrong*, 15/2.
wrett, pret., *wrote*, 69/9, 131/19.
writtare, n., *author*, 57/1, 67/22, 69/8.
wryttingis, n. pl., *letters*, 23/16; **writtingis**, 25/8.
ws, pron., *us*, 7/2.
wse, n., *use, custom*, 43/18.
wyiss, adj., *wise*, 11/3, 31/21, 113/6.
wyiss, n., *manner*, 167/7.

Ʒ

ʒeir, n., *year*, 5/12, 5/14; **ʒeiris**, pl., 5/20, 7/2, 13/15 etc.; **ʒeris**, 45/6.
ʒeirlie, adv., *annually*, 35/12.

ȝemanrie, n., *yeomanry*, 35/10.

ȝit, adv., conj., *still*, 27/20; ȝitt, 13/8, 25/6; *yet*, 3/10.

ȝow, pron., *you*, 3/12, 29/10, 29/15 etc.

ȝour, pron., *your*, 7/23, 9/17, 13/8 etc.; ȝowr, 93/14.

ȝouris, pron., *yours*, 19/1.

ȝung, adj., *young*, 29/8.